Marcus Aurelius'

MEDITATIONS FOR YOUNG MINDS

A Condensed Guide to Wisdom

Samuel Cartaxo

■■■

List of contributors: Marcus Aurelius, George Long

Meditations For Young Minds: A Condensed Guide to Wisdom

Part of this text is based on the wonderfully accurate works of George Long (1862) and John Jackson (1906), both in the public domain; however, it has been completely rewritten and expanded into contemporary language and style.

Edition/Version: 1/8 [Revised 19 April 2024]

1. Ethics.   2. Stoics.   3. Life.

■ ΑΩ ■

Expand your literary horizons and gift the joy of reading:
Discover a world of captivating books that inspire,
educate, and entertain!

https://www.legendaryeditions.art/

CONTENTS

INTRODUCTION — A Noble Emperor with Stoic Wisdom and Military Success 1

BOOK 1 — Living a Life of Compassion and Purpose 9

BOOK 2 — Discover a Meaningful Existence 13

BOOK 3 — Achieving Your Best Life 17

BOOK 4 — Harnessing Strength Within..............................21

BOOK 5 — Unlock Ancient Wisdom for Fulfillment 27

BOOK 6 — Open Your Path to Fulfillment...........................33

BOOK 7 — Be Kind, Be Virtuous, Be at Peace.......................41

BOOK 8 — Live in Harmony with Nature.............................49

BOOK 9 — Empower with Benevolence...............................57

BOOK 10 — Unveiling Your Inner Strength 63

BOOK 11 — The Journey of Self-Discovery..........................69

BOOK 12 — Embrace Life and Find Balance 75

GLOSSARY 81

INDEX 89

PREFACE

Welcome to "Meditations for Young Minds: A Condensed Guide to Wisdom." This book is a special adaptation of the Meditations by Marcus Aurelius, one of the most important works of philosophy and self-improvement ever written.

One of the unique features of this book is that it fills a crucial gap in the market for accessible and engaging works of philosophy aimed at younger readers. While there are many terrific books on philosophy and self-improvement available for adults, there are few resources specifically designed for young readers. "Meditations for Young Minds" seeks to address this gap by offering a simplified and condensed version of a classic work of philosophy that is accessible and engaging for young readers.

The Meditations are a collection of personal writings by Marcus Aurelius, who was a Roman Emperor and philosopher. In this work, he reflects on topics such as the nature of the universe, the importance of self-improvement, and the virtues of courage, justice, and wisdom. His thoughts and insights have been influential for centuries and continue to be studied and admired today.

In this book, we have taken the timeless wisdom of the Meditations and made it accessible to young readers. Each reflection or verse in the original text has been simplified and adapted for a younger audience, allowing readers to engage with Marcus Aurelius' teachings in a way that is easy to understand and apply to their own lives.

This book is a condensed guide to wisdom, offering valuable insights and guidance on how to live a virtuous and fulfilling life. Whether you are a young person looking to expand your knowledge and perspective, a teacher or parent seeking to introduce your students or children to philosophy, or simply someone who enjoys learning and self-improvement, this book has something for you.

By introducing young readers to philosophy at an early age, this book has the potential to inspire a new generation of thinkers and leaders. Philosophy can encourage critical thinking, empathy, and self-reflection, as well as instill important values like courage, justice, and wisdom. The text provides a bridge between classic works of philosophy and the modern reader, making it easier for young people to engage with important ideas and insights that have stood the test of time.

We hope that "Meditations for Young Minds" will inspire and enlighten you, and that the lessons contained within its pages will stay with you long after you have finished reading. Remember, the journey to wisdom and self-improvement is a lifelong one, and we are honored to be a part of it with you.

INTRODUCTION

— A Noble Emperor with Stoic Wisdom and Military Success

Born on April 26, A.D. 121, M. Annius Verus, from a noble family claiming descent from Numa, second King of Rome, would go on to be remembered as the most religious of all emperors. Both his parents had passed away too soon, yet Marcus held them dearly in his heart. His grandfather, the consular Annius Verus, adopted him and showed him deep love, from whom he learned to be gentle and meek, avoiding all anger and passion.

A Noble Emperor with Stoic Wisdom and Military Success

Marcus Annius Verus was born on April 26 in the year 121. He came from a noble family and was deeply religious. His parents died when he was young, but he was adopted by his grandfather who showed him lots of love. Marcus learned to be gentle and avoid getting angry or too emotional.

Rising Above Rome's Riots

The Emperor Hadrian saw that Marcus was a good person and called him "Verissimus," which means "more truthful than his own name." When Marcus was just eight years old, Hadrian made him a member of an important religious group. Later, Hadrian's daughter

Faustina was going to marry Marcus, so he was given a new name, Marcus Aurelius Antoninus.

He was taught to be profoundly serious about his education and to live a simple life. He learned a type of philosophy called Stoicism and was encouraged to be active, even though he could not do some of the more challenging activities because of his health.

In Rome, everyone was overly excited about the chariot races. But sometimes there was trouble because people got too excited and caused problems. Marcus did not get involved in the trouble, though.

The Rise of Marcus' Power

Marcus was an exceptionally talented person, and in 140 he became an especially important leader. Five years later, he got married and had a daughter. But Marcus wanted more, and soon he was given even more important titles. He was particularly important and seemed destined for greatness.

Challenges and Triumphs of an Emperor

After Antoninus Pius died, Marcus became the leader of the Roman Empire in 161. He chose Lucius Aurelius Verus to help him run things, with the plan for Verus to take over after Marcus. But right away, there were wars everywhere. Vologeses III from Parthia destroyed a Roman Legion and invaded Syria. Marcus sent Verus to fight him, but Verus got drunk and let his officers do the fighting.

Marcus had to deal with a big problem at home with some powerful tribes on the northern border. There were also diseases and floods in Rome that caused problems. Marcus had to sell some valuable things to get money and help with the famine. He and Verus fought against the tribes for a long time, but Verus died in 169.

The Roman forces won against the barbarian tribes, and Marcus' good choices for his team helped them win. In a battle against the Quadi, there was a legend that a Christian legion's prayers caused a storm that scared the barbarians and made them run away. This story is remembered in carvings in Rome.

After the settlement with the barbarian tribes, a man named Avidius Cassius tried to become emperor after Marcus died. Marcus quickly made peace and went to confront Cassius, but when he got there, Cassius' followers had already abandoned him. Cassius was killed by his own people, and Marcus refused to see the people who brought him Cassius' head.

The Loss of a Love and the Legacy of a Legend

After a tough journey, Marcus' wife Faustina died, but Marcus still celebrated a triumph. He then went to Germany and won a great victory, but it made him extremely sick. Sadly, he died from his illness in Pannonia in 180 A.D.

Emperor Marcus Aurelius had a tough time at home, with his wife Faustina losing many children. Only one son, Commodus, survived. When Marcus Aurelius died, Commodus became emperor, but he was not a good ruler and was cruel. Some people accused Faustina of being unfaithful and helping in a rebellion against Marcus, but there is no proof. Marcus loved his wife and there are still sculptures of them together.

The Virtuous Ruler

Marcus Aurelius was an incredibly good emperor who tried to do his best and be fair. He made some mistakes, but he also helped people by creating laws and charities to protect the weak and assist those in need. However, he was not particularly good to the Christians and did not seem to care about the bad things that happened to them. Overall, he was a good leader, but not perfect.

In ancient Rome, people did not find comfort in their religion, which was more about making deals with the gods than doing the right thing. Philosophies like Stoicism and Epicureanism became popular, both aiming for peace of mind. Stoics believed in controlling your emotions, while Epicureans sought freedom from troubles. Stoicism became famous for its resilience, while Epicureanism was associated with excess. We will focus on Stoicism.

Zeno of Cyprus was a philosopher born a long time ago who founded the Stoic school in Athens. He was well-traveled and met the Far East. Chrysippus, one of his students, helped organize Stoicism into a system and made it flourish. Chrysippus authored many books on Stoicism and is honored for his contributions.

But for Chrysippus, there had been no Porch

Zeno led the Stoics who believed in living in accordance with nature through Virtue. Philosophy was divided into three areas: Physics to explore the universe, Logic to recognize truth from falsehood, and Ethics to apply knowledge to daily life.

The Stoic Philosophy of Physics

The Stoics believed that only material objects were real, and rejected the Plato's belief that only ideas are real. However, they also believed that a spiritual force was at work in the material universe, which was shown through different forms like fire, spirit, soul, reason, and the governing principle.

The Stoics believed that the universe was made of material objects, but also had a spiritual force at work. They believed that popular deities were simply diverse ways of showing this spiritual force. Man's soul comes from this spiritual force and must eventually return to it. The universe works for everyone's benefit, but only virtue allows humans to work in harmony with it. The Stoics believed that living in accordance with nature and striving for virtue was the way to cooperate with the divine and achieve the highest good.

The Stoic Concept of Truth

The Stoics believed that our minds are like blank pages that get filled with ideas through our experiences. These experiences help us form general ideas and insights that help us understand the world.

Stoics believed that our experiences help us form ideas and insights. Some ideas are so strong that they cannot be denied, and they lead to truth. They thought that the best way to live is to be virtuous, which brings happiness. They believed that everything else, like health, wealth, and pleasure, does not matter as much as being virtuous.

The Stoics believed that being virtuous is the key to happiness. They believed that only virtue is good, and everything else, like health or wealth, is not important. The goal is to become a Wise Man who is happy and self-sufficient, even during challenging times. While nobody is perfect, the Stoics still aimed to be like the Wise Man.

Later Stoics recognized that not everything is either good or bad, but rather some things are preferable, and others are undesirable. They also believed that people who are not perfect can still do certain things that are neither good nor bad, but still important to do.

The Key Principles of Stoicism

The Stoics believed in two important principles. The first was to focus on what we can control, like our thoughts and feelings, and not worry about things we cannot control, like our health or reputation. They thought this was important because it helps us live in harmony with the universe. The second principle was to care about others and the world around us. This idea is like the Christian belief in a global community where everyone is equal and reminds us to live our lives in partnership with God.

The Stoic and Christian Philosophies

Marcus Aurelius was a philosopher and emperor who authored a book called Meditations. Even though he followed Stoic philosophy, his writing was not just about intellectual ideas, but a way to find inner peace and strength in the face of life's challenges. His words were gentle and full of wisdom, meant to comfort his own heart and inspire others on their journey through life.

The books "Meditations" and "Imitation of Christ" aim to teach people how to have self-control and peace of mind. They encourage us to focus on our own duties and not to let negative comments from others affect us. Both books emphasize the importance of community, and that life can be hard. They teach us to live our lives with virtue and passion.

The Imitation and the Meditations have diverse ways of helping people find peace of mind. The Imitation focuses on working with others and relying on God, while the Meditations are personal reflections from Marcus Aurelius. The Meditations give us a unique look into Marcus's thoughts, which are kind and focused on staying pure and avoiding negative emotions. He believes we should be polite and compassionate, even when someone hurts us.

Even when Marcus Aurelius struggles to live up to his own ideals, he remains committed to kindness and compassion. He teaches us that the best way to deal with wrongdoing is not to retaliate, but to respond with goodness. This is what makes his Meditations so special and unique.

Reflecting the Gentle Soul

Marcus Aurelius shows gratitude to the people who influenced his life, including his family, teachers, and mentors. He learned important qualities from each of them, such as kindness, courage, humility, piety, and generosity. His own goodness is reflected in the kindness he received from others, as he never held on to any negative feelings.

Marcus Aurelius had a strong and reliable heart like what Christians believe, but he did not have the same faith as them. He believed that there might be a God who governs the universe, or that things might just happen by chance. He thought that we can rely on our own judgement in important situations and that having a peaceful soul is important for a good life. He did not expect any special happiness beyond what we can find in this life.

He believed that our soul should prioritize being virtuous and trustworthy over our physical body. He did not care much about fame or wealth, considering them meaningless in the grand scheme of things. While he believed that the gods may watch over us, he felt that their primary concern was for the entire universe, and that should be enough.

Marcus Aurelius believed in divinities who were more involved in human matters than the Stoic divinities. He did not talk much about the afterlife, but he believed that his soul would eventually become part of the soul of the universe.

Marcus Aurelius had a quite different approach to life. He saw life as a battle that he had to fight until the end. He did not have a strong belief in an afterlife like Socrates did. Instead, he focused on doing his duty as a good person and hoped that his soul would eventually be absorbed into the universe.

The Search for Something Truer

Marcus Aurelius believed that his soul would be absorbed into the universe after his death. Despite accepting this intellectually, he still longed for something more. He wondered if there was another life after this one and if there were gods in that life too. He even considered the possibility that everything in this world was just a dream, and that there was something more real beyond it.

Marcus Aurelius admired nature's ability to regenerate from corruption and wondered if this power could be extended beyond physical things. He also had thoughts like St. Paul, and even mentioned Christians, albeit not in an incredibly positive light. As an emperor who valued the beauty of life, recognized the need for change, and searched for deeper truths, he left a legacy.

Sincerity Enables True Essence

Marcus Aurelius' Meditations are not complicated ideas, but he is honest about what he sees and feels.

Long ago, people used to follow religions that emphasized performing certain actions to appease the gods, rather than being good people with good intentions. The gods were more concerned with what people did than why they did it. Marcus Aurelius understood that a person's thoughts influence their behavior, and so he trained his soul in the right principles to be prepared for tricky situations.

Joy Beyond Pleasure

Marcus Aurelius understood that true happiness comes from having good intentions, virtuous desires, and righteous actions, rather than just seeking pleasure like some people believe. He realized that pleasure does not always lead to happiness and that being a good and virtuous person is more important.

Humble Warrior, Awe-Inspiring Sovereign

During the war, a humble and dutiful man rose to lead the Roman Empire. He foresaw the threat of barbarian invasions and successfully defended the Empire for two centuries.

Marcus Aurelius was a peaceful warrior and wise sovereign who sought simplicity and contentment. Despite his grandeur, he faced tragedy and lived a paradoxical life. He died while he was in a camp, in front of his enemies.

Timeline of Intellectual Curiosity

People have translated the writings of Marcus Aurelius for many years, which helps us understand him better. There have been many different translations over time, and they give us a clever idea about what he was like as a philosopher.

The writings of Marcus Aurelius help us understand what life was like a long time ago. They allow us to imagine and learn about his time in a fully accurate way.

BOOK 1

— Living a Life of Compassion and Purpose

Have compassion and purpose. We can take a lesson from Marcus' father, who emphasized the common humanity among people. By treating others with kindness, we can form meaningful relationships and strive for justice, thus making a positive impact on the world. Maintaining balance, avoiding trouble, and cherishing inner peace are crucial. With these principles in mind, we can lead a purposeful and satisfying life that benefits both ourselves and others.

1. A Legacy of Wisdom: Lessons from My Ancestors

My grandfather, Verus, taught me to be gentle, avoid anger, and be religious, while my mother taught me to be generous, abstain from evil, and eat simply. My great-grandfather advised me to attend public school and seek out good teachers.

2. A Wise Mentor's Advice: Navigating Between the Prasini and Veneti, Parmularii and Secutores

My mentor taught me to be a balanced person who avoids becoming obsessed with any one group and to stay away from trouble.

3. Unveiling a World of Wisdom: A Student's Journey with Diognetus

Diognetus taught me how to be smarter and more tolerant.

4. A Path to Redemption: My Journey with Rusticus

Rusticus introduced me to the notion that my life needed some sort of mending. He showed me that I did not need to be like the other sophists, and that I could be successful by writing letters without any pomp and reading extensively. He gave me a copy of Epictetus's Hypomnemata, for which I will always be grateful.

5. Witnessing the Wisdom of Apollonius: A Journey to True Liberty and Steadfastness

Apollonius was a great teacher who showed me how to be strong, independent, and humble.

6. Living the Life of Sextus: A Model of Moderation and Reason

Sextus was a kind, gentle man who was well-respected and had many friends. He was brilliant and knew how to live a good life.

7. The Art of Grammatical Correction: Tact and Delicacy

Following the teachings of Alexander, the Grammarian, I strive to speak flawlessly and never criticize another individual's mispronunciation or incorrect grammar. Instead, I aim to respond with tact and delicacy, affirming the sentiment while omitting the offending word. This way, I can inform the person of their mistake in a gentle and courteous manner.

8. Tyranny of the "eupatridai": A World of Deceit and Fraud

The regime of a despot king is exposed to a great degree of spite, shadiness, and pretentiousness. However, some people, known as "eupatridai," are sometimes incapable or deprived of natural fondness.

9. Cultivating Connections: Alexander the Platonic's Secret to Success

Alexander the Platonic was a busy man who always made time for his friends.

10. Unconditional Love: A Lesson Learned from Catulus' Entreaties

Even though Catulus is not always right, you will still try to be friends with him again.

11. Severus' Wisdom: Pursuing Justice and Philosophy with Kindness and Generosity

My dear brother Severus taught me many things, including how to be kind, loving, and determined to create a just society.

12. The Uprightness of Claudius Maximus: A Legacy of Wisdom and Strength

Claudius Maximus was a wise, honorable man who always approached his tasks with vigor and determination. He was kind and courteous, and always in good humor. He was a model of high moral character and integrity, and his word was always respected.

13. A Beacon of Resilience: My Father's Unwavering Spirit

My father was a model of meekness, constancy, impartiality, wisdom, temperance, generosity, care for his own body, and respect for true philosophers.

14. Living According to Nature: A Blessing from the Gods

The gods blessed me with good family, friends, and servants. I never mistreated them. My father taught me that a prince can live simply. I had a brother who inspired me. My children are healthy. I helped those in need and always had the means to do so. I have a wife and was able to choose good caretakers for my children. I had useful dreams. I studied philosophy wisely. All this was thanks to the gods and fortune.

15. United by Nature: Recognizing Our Kinship

We are all brothers and sisters, and it's best not to get angry with one another.

16. The Human Paradox: A Journey of Reason and Being

Be mindful of your being, and trust in your destiny.

17. Unveiling the Web of Divine Benevolence

The gods cause everything, and we should be grateful for their benevolence.

BOOK 2

— Discover a Meaningful Existence

Make the most of every moment and take charge of your life. To live a fulfilling life, it is essential to avoid immoral actions and focus on embracing life rather than fearing death. Living in the present moment is vital, and gaining understanding of others' beliefs and assumptions can bring clarity and inner peace. By adopting these principles, you can discover a deeper sense of purpose and satisfaction in your daily existence.

1. Awaken to Life's Reality: Seize the Day!

Wake up and do what you are supposed to do today! It is your chance to make a difference!

2. Living a Divine Life: The Roman Way

Live a good life, be serious, and do not be a jerk.

3. Take Control of Your Life: Time Waits for No Man

Soul, rise and take control! Respect yourself, and do not wait for others to tell you what to do. Time is running out, so act now!

4. Don't Waste Time Roaming Aimlessly: Take Time to Learn Something Worth Knowing

Learn something worth knowing, and do not let external events distract you.

5. Neglecting Compassion: A Recipe for Misery

Those who fail to consider others' inner state may experience true misery. Wisdom and prudence are necessary to guide one's own soul and avoid unhappiness.

6. Unlock the Power of Cosmic Understanding

The Cosmos is vast and mysterious, and it is full of exciting things to explore. You are a part of it all, and you have the power to be effective. So, use your abilities to help make the world a better place.

7. Enthusiastic Sins: More Condemned than Angry Ones?

Sinners who sin out of pleasure are worse than those who sin out of anger.

8. Behold the Greatest Gift: Embrace Life, Fear Not Death

Live each day as if it were your last, and you will be blessed with a brave and fearless heart.

9. The Transience of Life: A Reflection

Think about how everything changes and disappears over time. Everything is temporary, including us.

10. Honor and Esteem in the Face of Death

Death is a natural process that is both beneficial and inevitable. It is important to understand it as part of nature to avoid fear and embrace life.

11. Searching for the Divine Within

We are all connected to God in some way, and the best way to serve is to keep ourselves free from turbulent emotions, rash behavior, and senseless pride.

12. Living in the Present: The Same for Every Lifetime

Remember that the present is all we have, and that when we die, we part with the present and go to the future.

13. The Sweet Adventure of Life

All opinions and assumptions are just that – opinions and assumptions. It is important to take them seriously and consider their potential uses.

14. Apostasy from Nature: A Man's Self-Inflicted Detriment

Sinful behavior leads to spiritual harm and disaster. A man's soul can be harmed in many ways, and it is important to avoid them.

15. The Unfailing Power of Philosophy

Philosophy is the most important thing in life because it gives us a sense of perspective and peace.

BOOK 3

— Achieving Your Best Life

Embrace the values that truly matter. Take charge of your time and live with purpose by seizing every opportunity. Find value in the world around you and derive meaning from your daily routines. Foster self-sufficiency, uphold integrity, and prioritize honesty over deception. By avoiding excess and maintaining a consistent exercise routine, you can achieve contentment in life and become a more mindful and responsible caretaker of the environment.

1. Time Is Running Out: Make the Most of What You Have Left

You must use your time wisely and act quickly, or your mind will slowly fade, and you will lose your ability to think, reason and make wise choices.

2. The Profundity of Nature: Seeing Beyond Beauty

Appreciate the beauty of nature by looking beyond the obvious.

3. The End of the Journey: Life, Sense and Mortality

Some people died in accidents, some in wars, and some of natural causes. Some people predicted to die did not die as predicted, while others who were not predicted to die died unexpectedly.

4. Living a Life of Purposeful Thought

Do not let your life be taken up by pondering over others, who have no connection to the greater good. Avoid thinking about what someone is doing, saying, or thinking, or any other irrelevant, nosy notions. Train yourself to think only of those topics that you would not feel ashamed to admit to another. If you can do this, it will be clear that you are sincere and peaceable, and that you do not prioritize pleasure or let yourself be tempted by any voluptuous ideas. You should be free from all conflict, envy, and suspicion. Put off the lesser and focus on the best, and become a minister of the gods, in full accord with your inner self.

5. Living with Honor: A Call to Action

Follow the advice of your elders and do what you think is best for yourself. Be confident and honest with others.

6. Be Your Own Guide to Contentment

Be independent, honest, and upright, and do not let others sway your decisions.

7. The True Path to Enlightenment: Rejecting Deception and Sensuality

In this life, pursue righteousness, truth, temperance, fortitude, and contentment more than anything else – for nothing is greater than the spirit within. Avoid temptation, withdraw from sensuality, and care for all while submitting to the gods. Do not let honor, riches, or pleasure compete with what is rational and good. Choose what benefits you as a rational being, and discard what only benefits you as a creature. See things as they truly are by ignoring deceptive appearances. Follow your heart, mind, and spirit, and you will be happy.

8. The Path to a Life of Dignity: Prioritize Your Rational Spirit

Be honest and truthful, and you will never have to worry about hurting anyone's feelings or betraying your trust.

9. A Perfect Performance: The Disciplined Mind

If you practice rigorously and clean your mind, you will be free of any corrupting thoughts or emotions, and your life will be full and complete.

10. Unlock Your Potential: A Reflection on Our Place in the Universe

Think before you speak, be respectful, and live life to the fullest.

11. Unveiling the World's Secrets Through Mindful Observation

Use your observational skills to learn about the world around you and appreciate the details that make it a fascinating place.

12. Unveiling the Almighty's Gifts: Making Sense of Life's Choices

Things in life are temporary but are still subject to the will of the Almighty. We should be benevolent and just to those around us, regardless of their rank or position.

13. The Path to Contentment: Embark Now!

Seek truth, be rational and stay humble on your journey to find happiness.

14. Leveraging Both Divine and Human Knowledge: A Key to Success

Always have your tools ready because you never know when you will have to use them.

15. Be Wise, Hasten to a Conclusion: A Call to Self-Preservation

Do not deceive yourself. You will not live long enough to read all the books you have saved for your old age, including moral reflections and works by famous Greeks and Romans. So, hurry up and let go of any unrealistic expectations. Take care of yourself while you still can.

16. Exploring the Depths of Mind, Body, and Spirit

We have a body, soul and mind like everyone else, but what makes a good person special is that he is happy with whatever happens, keeps his mind calm, always acts with truth and justice, stays on the right path, no matter what others think. Take what comes without complaining and be at peace with whatever fate brings.

17. The Path to Integrity: Accepting Life's Role with Contentment

Be content with who you are and what you have. Ignore the people who try to make you change.

BOOK 4

— Harnessing Strength Within

To overcome life's challenges, we must first cultivate a strong internal foundation. To live a fulfilling life, we must accept ourselves and our situations, and have the strength to face challenges with resilience. Simplifying our lives and focusing on the present can help us achieve our goals and be content. Being kind to others and pursuing our passions with purpose is also important. We should remember that our time is limited and strive to make the most of it. By embracing the vastness of the universe and our role in it, we can find motivation to pursue our dreams and live life to the fullest.

1. Unbounded by Obstacles: The Strength of the Human Spirit

The human spirit is adaptable and can adjust to achievable goals when the original ones become unattainable. It does not limit itself to one objective and remains flexible in pursuing its goals. Challenges strengthen it, just like a fire that grows stronger as it burns through obstacles.

2. Crafting Perfection: A Guide

Do not act hastily or randomly, but rather follow the precise and flawless principles of art in all things.

3. Seeking Peace in the Depths of Your Soul

When you need a break, take it. Reflect on the transient nature of the world and appreciate all that life has to offer.

4. A Unified Global Civilization: Our Common Point of Origin

The law that dictates what is right and wrong is universal and comes from understanding.

5. Acceptance of the Inevitable: Generation and Death

Nature is constantly creating and destroying, and we must accept it as part of our reality.

6. Futility of Denial: The Inevitable End

Life is full of hard truths, so do not be surprised if the things you think will happen do not.

7. The Inevitability of Neutrality

The axiom of human experience is that, when our ability to judge is stripped away, we cannot be wronged.

8. Life Is Equitable: Act Accordingly

Pay attention to what is happening, and you will see that it is happening in a logical and fair way.

9. Reality Check: Don't be Fooled

Do not be a victim and do not let anyone manipulate you into thinking they are right. Look at the situation critically and figure out what is really going on.

10. Uplifting Mankind: A Moral Compass for Action

Remember to take care when making decisions and be open to the latest information if it could lead to a better outcome.

11. Reason: Use It or Lose It!

If you have a good reason for doing something, you do not need a reason to do it.

12. The Cycle of Creation and Dissolution

You will eventually be absorbed back into your creator.

13. Ascension to Divinity in 9 Days

You will become a deity in a week and a half.

14. Live Now: The Clock is Ticking

Live your life to the fullest and make the most of every moment.

15. Stay the Course: Reap the Rewards

Achievement is born of focus, and it is the best way to achieve your goals.

16. The Futility of Praise: Beauty Exists Beyond Praise

In the end, all memory will be extinguished, so whatever is beautiful or good does not need praise to make it so.

17. Unveiling the Mystery of the Afterlife: A Journey of Discovery

The earth contains the remains of the buried because they are converted into air, fire, and blood. Souls may linger after death, and we can learn something about the material world from examining how animals are consumed and buried.

18. Seeking Justice in Every Thought

Do not stray from the path of righteousness because doing so will lead to justice. Be mindful of what you think and feel, so you can make wise decisions.

19. A Love Song for the World

The World is a beautiful place, and I am happy to enjoy every moment of it.

20. Cut the Clutter: Simplify Your Life!

Simplify your life by focusing on the necessary actions and thoughts.

21. Live Wisely and Enjoy Every Moment!

Life is short, so enjoy it while you can.

22. The Art of Serendipity: A Mystery Unveiled

Can this world be a beautiful work of art or exquisite chaos? Each part is unique yet linked together. Is it serendipitous and still gorgeous? The answer remains unknown.

23. The Unbearable Inanity of Human Nature

Life is full of disappointments, but do not give up on yourself.

24. Simplify and Prioritize: A Guide to Finding Tranquility

Rather than only focusing on a few things to find tranquility as philosophers advise, we should prioritize doing what is necessary and fulfilling our social duties, as this brings both tranquility from doing things well and peace from doing less. A lot of what we do is unnecessary, so by eliminating superfluous actions and thoughts, we free up time, reduce stress, and prevent further unnecessary actions. By simplifying life to just the essentials and focusing only on what truly matters, we can embrace a tranquil existence full of peace and calm.

25. A Half-Naked Philosopher: Seeking Instruction to Feed the Mind and Soul

Even though I am not well-clothed and without food, I still pursue knowledge because it is the best way to stay alive and happy.

26. Live Life with Purpose and Compassion

Embrace your chosen craft or career and savor it; surrender the rest of your life to the divine and treat your fellow humans with kindness and respect.

27. Time Marches On: Reflecting on the Folly of Life

The times of Vespasian, Trajan, and other rulers are all the same – some marry, some raise children, some sick, some die, some war, some feast, some trade, some farm, some flatter, some brag, some distrust, some plot, some wanting to die, some grumble, some woo, some hoard, some seek power, some seek kingdoms. But do not worry – someday, the times of these rulers will end, and the times of other eras will begin. Think of the people you know in life and remember to do what is appropriate for their importance and measure.

28. Nothing Lasts Forever: Accepting Fate and Embracing Life's Journey

Things that we once took for granted will soon be gone, but we should focus on what we can control and make the most of our time.

29. The Universe of Transformation: A Reflection

The universe is continually changing, and that includes everything that exists. Be happy that everything is constantly evolving because that means that we can all grow and learn together.

30. The Road Ahead: Seeking True Simplicity and Meekness

Death is a scary thing, but there is nothing to worry about. You will get there eventually.

31. The Wise Ones: Revealed in Fear & Desire

The world deems those who are wise to be those who flee from things in terror. But the wise see what others flee from and crave it.

32. The Transcendence of Suffering: A Journey to Peace

Suffering will only make you suffer more if you focus on it, so do not think about it. Just focus on your soul and you will be fine.

33. The Unified Force of Life: A Marvelous Tapestry

Behold the world, a single entity, connected and intertwined in all its parts. Everything works in harmony, driven by a single unified force. All things rely on each other and marvel at the intricate tapestry of cause and effect that holds this universe together.

34. A Wretched Soul Carrying a Carcass

Life is hard, but it is worth it.

35. Embrace the Currents of Change

Change is the key to life, and progress is the key to happiness.

36. The Unseen Symphony of Life

The world is a beautiful and orderly place, and we can learn a lot by looking at it closely.

37. Reasoning for Ourselves: Unraveling Heraclitus' Insight

Think for yourself and do not blindly follow what others say or do.

38. One Day or a Thousand: The Value of Time

Do not be distressed by the thought of death – it will come to everyone in the end. Focus instead on living each day to the fullest and enjoying the present moment.

39. A Speck of Snivel: Reflecting on Life's Transience

Reflect on the life of man and appreciate the moment we are in.

40. Unbowed in the Storm

You must never give up on yourself, no matter how hard things get. You can always find a way to overcome whatever challenges come your way.

41. The Art of Finding Happiness in Misfortune

Although something bad has happened to me, I do not feel very unhappy because I am able to go on in the same way as before. I am still just, magnanimous, temperate, wise, circumspect, true, modest, and free.

42. The Infinite Abyss: Taking Life in Stride

Life is short, enjoy it while you can.

43. The Freedom of Nature's Path: A Guide to Living Life Well

You need to try to do things the way nature does them if you want to be happy and successful.

BOOK 5

— Unlock Ancient Wisdom for Fulfillment

Take charge of your life! Explore the guidance of ancient philosophers for a fulfilling life. Embrace philosophy for comfort, hope, and purpose. Develop reason, emotional control, and empathy. Respect the universe and embrace nature. Use these tools to live a satisfying life, even during tough times. Begin living your best life and making a positive impact on the world.

1. Rise and Strive: What is one's Nature's Purpose?

Be devoted to your purpose and deny yourself sleep and food if necessary to achieve it.

2. Achieve Tranquility: The Simple Solution

It is easy to relax and be at peace when you remove all distractions from your mind.

3. Embrace Nature's Call, Ignore Others' Judgment

Follow your natural instincts and do not be afraid to stand up for what you believe in. People will criticize you, but do not let that discourage you.

4. Sustained by the Earth: A Final Exhale

Life is a cycle of rebirth and death. We are all born, we all die. But we can control how we live our lives, by obeying the laws of nature. When we are gone, our air will still be around, and the earth will still be there to sustain us.

5. Achieving Greatness, Despite Limitations: The Choice is Yours!

You cannot help your natural limitations, but you can still be successful if you work hard and have good character.

6. Do Good Deeds Without Expectation

Some people believe that virtuous deeds need to be acknowledged to be recognized as good, but that is not always necessary. What is important is the deed itself. So, if you want to do a good deed, go ahead and do it without worrying about whether people will applaud you.

7. Prayers of Generosity: A Supplication

When you pray, be sincere and humble.

8. Accepting Destiny's Curveballs: For the Universe's Sake

Just as doctors prescribe different treatments to achieve a person's health, so too does the universe prescribe illness, blindness, or some other kind of loss or damage to us. We should accept these things as necessary for the coherence and continuity of the whole.

9. The Comforting Embrace of Philosophy: Don't Lose Hope

Do not give up on your efforts, even if it is sometimes difficult. Do not begrudge the distractions of the world or the weaknesses of human nature. Philosophy does not ask more of you than what your nature does, and why would you choose something that goes against nature? Magnanimity, freedom, modesty, composure, and holiness are all kinder and more natural than pleasure, which can be so destructive.

10. Live Life Without Fear: Embrace the Inevitable

Console yourself in anticipation of your inevitable death, but do not worry about it coming too late. Accept that nothing happens to you that is not part of the universe's grand plan, and you are powerless to do anything that would be against your own values. You have no control over being forced to do something in which you do not believe.

11. Unlocking the Intention of Your Spirit

The use you are now making of your soul is important. You should ask yourself this question on all occasions.

12. The Noble and the Base: What Is Truly Good?

The things that are genuinely good are wise and good for the community.

13. The Unending Journey of Transformation

I am an eternal being that exists in many different forms and changes over time.

14. The Power of the Achievements: Rejecting the External for Self-Fulfillment

Reason and rational capacity are faculties that content themselves with their own operations and their primary goal is to arrive at a plausible result.

15. Coloring Your Mind: The Path to Happiness through Rationality

Think about what you want to achieve in life and strive to get there. Remember that everyone has potential, and that everyone is working towards the same goal. Society is a valuable asset, and those with sagacious essence are the most important.

16. The Immeasurable Power of Choice

Sometimes things happen that we cannot control, but it is important to stay hopeful and try to do what is best for ourselves.

17. Taming the Neutral Force: Overcoming Obstacles with Determination

I view humans as a neutral force, just like the sun, wind, or a wild animal. These entities may obstruct my actions, but my mind and determination cannot be blocked, for it is equipped with a perpetual capacity for exceptions and transformations. If a barrier arises, my mind will convert it into the focus of my work, turning the obstacle into the quickest route to achieving my aims.

18. Honoring the Universal Force Within

Show respect for the highest authority in the universe by paying tribute to it. This power is within all of us and can help us change the world around us for the better.

19. The Transience of Life: Embrace It Wisely

Do not get caught up in the petty squabbles of the world. Remember that everything will eventually pass away, and that you are just a tiny part of something much larger. Stay focused on your own nature, and do not let anyone else control or distract you. Everything will work out in the end.

20. Embrace the Natural: A Guide to Emotional Discipline

When you feel physical pain or pleasure, try to ignore them, and focus on your soul. If they get too close, accept them as part of nature, but do not attach any value to them.

21. Embracing Fate's Divine Plan

The person lives a divine life and is always content and delighted. They are happy to embrace whatever fate the Spirit has decreed for them.

22. Gently Guide, Don't Fume: A Call for Compassion

Do not be angry when someone has bad breath or armholes.

23. Live Freely: The Power of Choice

If you cannot live with the people who are around you, you can find a better place to live by being autonomous and free.

24. The Hidden Harmony of the Universe

The universe is a wonderful place that makes everything work out for the best.

25. A Life Well-Lived: Reflections on a Journey Completed

You have been a great person, and you will continue to be one even in your final days.

26. Unlocking the Wisdom of the Ages

The wise and prudent person knows what they are doing, and they should not be messed with. They are the one who understands the start and finish of anything, and they have the insight of a rational spirit that exists throughout everything. They can direct and manage this universe to a certain degree of time.

27. A Moment of Transience: What Now?

Do not cling to things that will inevitably end. Cling to things that will last.

28. The Pursuit of Justice: A Path to True Contentment

Be true to yourself and your goals, and you will be on the right track.

29. The Noise of Court: A Tale of Fools

Do not worry about what others think and focus on what is important.

30. Ready to Die, Ready to Live: Destiny

Death may come at any time, but it is not always a bad thing. In fact, some people are happy even when they die.

31. Creating One's Own Fortune: A Blessing of the Spirit

To be able to create your own happiness and fortune is an incredibly lucky thing. You can thank your lucky stars for this blessing each and every day!

BOOK 6

— Open Your Path to Fulfillment

Embrace the benevolence of the universe! Accept the natural flow of life and find contentment in the present. Remember that life is fleeting, so make each moment count. Live with intention and compassion, facing challenges with virtue and kindness. Acknowledge the interdependence of all things and develop an appreciation for the natural world. Show reverence for the environment and all its inhabitants. Place value on knowledge, logic, and intellectual growth. Look to the teachings of great philosophers and leaders and incorporate their wisdom into your daily existence. You hold the ability to make a positive impact on the world. Use this ability thoughtfully and live a life that brings pride.

1. The All-Encompassing Benevolence of the Universe

The universe is kind, omnipotent, and nothing can hurt us.

2. Death or Duty: A Call to Action

Whatever you do, do your best. You cannot change what is happening, but you can control how you react to it.

3. Unfathomable Worth: Look Within

Do not let anything pass you by until you understand it.

4. The Inexplicable Nature of Transformation

Life is a mystery that we can never fully understand.

5. Standing Above the Conflict: Preserving Dignity

Stand tall and do not let bullies get you down.

6. A Path of Kindness: God's Blessing

Do virtuous deeds and God will be with you.

7. The Masterful Architect of Fate

The intellectual overseer is a powerful being that can control its own destiny and create its own environment. Everything that happens is revealed to it in a way that it chooses.

8. A Higher Power: Navigating the Universe's Mysteries

To understand the universe, you must understand its nature.

9. Reset and Reharmonize

When life gets tough, remember to come back to yourself and regain your composure.

10. Persevering with Dual Motherhood: Court and Philosophy as Refuge

Honor and respect both your stepmother and your biological mother but be especially close to your biological mother.

11. Illusions of Grandeur: Stripped Away

The things we eat, drink, and wear are all just things. Sex is just people rubbing against each other and producing stuff. And imagine being able to see through all the illusions that life throws at us!

12. Crates' Insights on Xenocrates: Impressive Wisdom and Inspiring Ideas

Xenocrates was a great philosopher, and his ideas were especially important.

13. Exploring the Divine Rationality

People are fascinated by things like stones, timber, figs, and vines. Some people take joy in the living, while others admire only the rational. The one who honors a reasonable spirit at its core, for its reasonableness and its sociability, looks past everything else to protect their own.

14. A Moment in Time

Life is fleeting, and we cannot hold on to anything.

15. Contentment Found: Natural Constitution?

We should strive to be content with what our natural constitution allows us and focus on becoming happy in this life.

16. Following the Path of Virtue

The motion of virtue is a difficult path, but it leads to success and prosperity.

17. Chasing an Unattainable Dream

The idea of wanting to be appreciated by future generations is puzzling.

18. Reach Beyond the Impossible

If you can imagine it, you can do it.

19. The Palestra's Wisdom: Stay Away, Without Hatred

When you get beaten in the palestra, do not hold a grudge, just try to save yourself.

20. Seeking the Truth: No Harm Done

Mistakes are a sign that you are trying, and that is a good thing.

21. Trust in the Gods, Act with Kindness

Be kind, do what is right, and have faith.

22. Equal Fates: All Things Unite

Everything in the world is made up of the same things, and when somebody dies, they eventually go back to where they came from or are broken down into their most basic elements.

23. Uncountable Universes in One

The universe is a big place with a lot of stuff happening.

24. Spell It Out: Antoninus

If someone challenges you about how to spell Antoninus, you can respond in a sequence of letters or numbers, to reach your desired outcome.

25. A Tough Choice: Help or Deny?

Be patient with those who do not follow your chosen path, it is their own doing.

26. Ceasing Sensory Tyranny and Mind Error

Death is the end of everything that is bad in life.

27. Live Meaningfully: The Philosopher's Way

Do not let your body outlast your soul. Live a life of virtue and meaning.

28. Pius' Path to Peace

Antoninus Pius was a great Emperor. He was unwavering in his commitment to logic, even-tempered, holiness, brightness of face, graciousness, and humility. He was a successful scholar who was willing to listen to all sides and refused to be swayed by unsubstantiated claims or fearmongering. He was also content with simple comforts and worked hard. Antoninus Pius was loyal to friends and committed to being challenged. He was also pious and had a pure, unadulterated faith.

29. Dream-Seeking in Reality

Do not take things too seriously when you are dreaming.

30. One Unified Being: Neutrality, Presentism, and Beyond

Our bodies and minds are the same, and we should not be concerned with things that do not concern us.

31. The Paradox of Pleasure

People who enjoy pleasure in life are usually criminals, and it is not good for them.

32. Reverence of Craft Over Reason

Behold, even those that practice mundane skills, who could be considered as simpletons, remain devoted to their craft.

33. One Source, Many Forms

Everything, big or small, good, or bad, comes from the same source, and time is both still and constantly changing.

34. One Interconnected World

All things are related and intertwined, so look at the present and appreciate everything that exists.

35. Living in Nature's Harmony

Make the most of the people and circumstances you are with and follow the natural intentions of things. Everything will work out in the end.

36. Focus on Our Will, Not Fate

Do not focus on things you cannot control and be grateful for what you can.

37. Our Role in the Grand Plan

You have a role to play in the world, and it is important to take a moment to consider what it is. You are not just a cog in a machine, you are part of something greater.

38. A Celestial Symphony: Uncovering the Bigger Picture

The sun, rain and earth all have different jobs to do, and the stars are all working together to make things happen.

39. Obedience to the Gods: My Duty, My Choice

The gods can have any opinion they want, but I decide what is best for me, even if that means going against what the gods want. I will always try to be kind and rational, and I will love my homeland of Rome even if I never visit it.

40. Collective Betterment: The "Neutral" Expedient

In the grand scheme of things, everything happens for a reason, and it is ultimately for the good of everyone.

41. Breaking the Cycle: A New Hope

Life is a never-ending cycle of the same events, the same sights, the same emotions.

42. Speak Meekly: The Value of Life

Remember that death is always around us, and that it is a natural part of life. However, remember that there is much to value in life, even if it is short.

43. A Mosaic of Humanity – Cherish It

Reflect upon the admirable traits of those around you and keep them in your thoughts always.

44. Accepting Your Limited Poundage and Years: Finding Contentment

Remember that you have only a finite amount of time, so be happy with what you have.

45. Achieving the Impossible: Temper Your Desires

Persuade others even if they are adamantly opposed and be content with any results. Remember that you do not have to achieve something impossible to be happy.

46. Wisdom Lies in Self-Action

Be happy with what you do, not with what other people think of it.

47. Unchain Yourself from Emotional Tethers

You can free your mind of any thoughts or emotions connected to this topic by simply not thinking about them.

48. Be Present, Listen Deeply

Listen carefully and focus on what the person is saying. Let go of other thoughts and be present in the moment.

49. The Bee's Dilemma

The bee is always looking out for the best interests of its hive and will do whatever it takes to ensure its success.

50. The Voyage of Uncertainty

We are all anxious about our journey and what will happen to us while we are on it. We are also concerned with how our caretakers will treat us.

51. Gone Too Soon: Reflections on Mortality

Many people who were born at the same time as you are already gone.

52. The Power of Perceived Truths

Believe in yourself, and you will be able to face any challenge.

53. Unhindered Nature: Live Freely

You are responsible for your life, and no one can stop you from doing what is best for you.

54. Time's Unforgiving Nature

The people in the world are trying to please different people, and they want to achieve different things. Time will pass quickly and bury all things.

BOOK 7

— Be Kind, Be Virtuous, Be at Peace

Stay true to your beliefs, as wickedness is familiar. Your worth is based on your feelings, so be thoughtful about what you say. Do your best with what you have, trust yourself, and be peaceful about the uncertain future. Remember, physical things will disappear, but abstract things will remain. Be natural and logical in your actions since everything is unstable. Be kind and true to yourself, do not change to fit in, and find comfort in understanding. Happiness comes from being virtuous and knowing your place. Death and change are natural, so forgive and let go. Focus on the present, be kind, and live in the moment. Acting with virtue is noble, so stand up for what is right and appreciate beauty. We can learn from the past to make the world better. Stay positive, determined, and strive for excellence.

1. An Endless Cycle of Familiarity

Wickedness is something that has been seen, known and experienced countless times before.

2. Unfazed by the Unknown: Find Joy in Understanding

Stay true to your beliefs and you will be happy.

3. Living Again: A Man's Worth is His Affections

Live a life centered around your affections, and you will be worth everything.

4. Unraveling the Language of Truth

Do not just say things because everyone else is saying them. Carefully think about what you are saying and why.

5. Climbing the Wall of Success: Alone or with an Ally?

I will try to do the best I can, with the resources I have.

6. Finding Harmony in the Universe

The future is always uncertain, but that is okay. Everything will work out in the end. There is one order, one God, one truth for all reasonable creatures. So, trust in yourself and be at peace.

7. Fame and Memory: A Cosmic Ephemerality

Everything that exists in the physical world will eventually disappear, while the abstract things that animate the physical will be absorbed into the greater understanding of the universe. In the end, all that remains is the passage of time.

8. Reason and Nature Unite

Actions are according to nature if they happen naturally, and actions are according to reason if they make sense.

9. Everything is unstable, it cannot be corrected

Straight of itself, not made straight.

10. Love for All: The Joy of Kindness

Remember that you are a part of a larger community, and that it is only when you act with kindness that you truly start to understand the joy of life.

11. Unharmed by Fate's Fickle Fortune

Do not let the cosmos sway you, it is not under your control. Be brave and try not to think of events as unlucky.

12. My Integrity, My Colorful Shining Jewel

Resist the temptation to change who you are to fit in or to please others. Remember that you are the only person who can be true to yourself, and that will make you stand out in a clever way.

13. My Mind, My Strength, My Refuge

The understanding is a safe and comforting place, free from fear and sadness.

14. The Search for Happiness: Unveiled

Happiness is knowing your place in the world and not needing others.

15. Embracing Change: Necessary to Life's Existence

Change is a part of life. You cannot go through life without it. Death is also a part of life. You must expect it.

16. Uncovering the Grand Organism: A Journey of Discovery

Every living thing is connected to each other, and we are all part of a bigger picture. Keep your focus on what is important, and be kind to others, no matter what they do.

17. The Transient Nature of Existence

The cycle of life and death is a natural law of the universe.

18. Renewal Amidst the Fervor: The Cycle of Reason

Know when to let go.

19. Forgiveness: Our Common Humanity

Be mindful of your actions and try to understand why someone did what they did. If you can do this, you can forgive them.

20. Embrace the Present: Find Inner Peace

Stay focused on the present, and do not get too carried away with what you hope the future will bring. You will be happier that way.

21. Unleash the Power of Reflection

The important things in life are exploring and learning, being kind and loving, and living now.

22. The Impermanence of Death: A Journey of Release

Life is ordered and predetermined, and everything is quickly forgotten. Death is a relief and a means of transformation. Pain is soon ended by death, and what lasts long can be bearable. Meanwhile, the mind can maintain its serenity by cutting off all communication and sympathy with the body.

23. A Grand Mind's Perspective on Death: Tragedy or Not?

Immense intellects do not think of death as a misfortune because they are focused on the bigger picture.

24. Beauty of the Mind: A Noble Pursuit

Acting with virtue is a true mark of nobility, even if it is met with criticism. Our minds should be given the same attention as our bodies and be sculpted and groomed in a way that best reflects our innermost selves.

25. The Cornfield of Life: Standing Tall Despite Fate's Hand

Life is a cornfield, and while it may be difficult, we must not despair. We must fight for what is right, and never give up.

26. Living Honorably Despite the Chaos: Embracing Life's Perplexity

Live a life of virtue and good character and appreciate the beauty of the universe around you.

27. The Inevitable Cycle of Time

The past, present, and future are all part of the same cycle – we cannot control what happens, but we can learn from it. Everything will eventually wind down and go back to the way it was before.

28. Strength vs. Compassion: Who Wins?

No one is perfect, but people who are kind, generous, and forgiving are the kind of people who make the world a better place.

29. The Power of Optimism: Rewarding Ourselves through Righteous Actions

No matter what life throws our way, we can remain positive and determined, and reap the rewards of our actions.

30. Unwavering Vision, Unequivocal Focus

Strive for excellence in everything you do, and you will be on your way to a fulfilling life. Keep your focus on what is important, and you will be successful.

31. Embrace Life's Adversities and Thrive

Live your life to the fullest. Embrace the challenge, remember the people who have gone before you, and do not give up on your dreams.

32. Achieving Dignified Poise: A Guide

You need to use your mind and body to stay still and focused to be a successful person. Be yourself, without trying to be someone else.

33. Mastering Life's Struggles: A Necessary Skill

Stay strong and fight through everything life throws at you, so you can be a successful person.

34. Uncovering Unspoken Truths: A Guide

Be understanding and kind to everyone, no matter what they think or feel.

35. Pain Is Not the Boss of You!

Do not be ashamed of your pain and remember that it is temporary. It is also okay to be unhappy occasionally – remember that pain has gotten the better of me.

36. The Danger of Unnatural Affections

If you stand around people who do bad things, you might get like them.

37. Unraveling Socrates' Soul: The Ultimate Inquiry

Socrates was a great man because he had a great soul, and he did not let the things that happened to him get him down.

38. Achieving Spiritual Fulfillment Without Recognition

It is possible to be spiritual and remain unknown, but it is important to remember that true contentment is rare. Even if you do not achieve success in one area of your life, do not lose hope in the other areas.

39. Embracing Life's Unexpected Challenges

The present moment is a gift from God, and you should use it to achieve your goals.

40. Living Perfectly: A Journey of Passion and Balance

Aim to be your best self and be honest and genuine in your relationships.

41. A Sinner's Dilemma: Eternal Patience, Momentary Complaints

Gods must feel incredibly happy enduring with us sinners for 10,000 years. We are grateful for their care, but we should try to be better people ourselves.

42. Ignoring the Unpleasurable and Unlovable

Our rational and convivial faculty ignores objects that do not give us pleasure or offer us opportunities for love.

43. Be Kind and Reap the Rewards

Acts of kindness bring us the greatest rewards.

44. The Universe's Grand Design: A Moment of Peace

The Universe has a plan, and everything that has happened is a part of it.

BOOK 8

— Live in Harmony with Nature

Take control of your life and find true contentment by living in line with nature's principles. Focus on your aspirations while considering the impact of your actions on others. Embrace change and view obstacles as opportunities to pursue your purpose. Balance your perspective by considering the broader picture. Speak humbly and respectfully, trusting that your actions will benefit humanity. Accept that everything is impermanent and cherish life's fleeting nature. Be kind to yourself when things do not go as planned. You possess the ability to reach your full potential and make a positive impact. Take action to improve the world and seize every opportunity. Avoid complaining and make the most of your time.

1. Find True Contentment: Live by Nature's Principles

Concentrate on understanding what your nature desires and living for that purpose. Everything else will follow.

2. Reasonable Actions for the Common Good: A Final Reflection

Ask yourself if what you are doing is in the best interest of others.

3. A Tale of Two Paths: Alexander, Caius, Pompeius vs. Diogenes, Heraclitus, and Socrates

The three wise men differed in their understanding of the world and what it means to be human.

4. Living Life in the Grand Scheme: The Impermanence of Our Existence

Do not be a jerk, be kind, and enjoy life while you can.

5. The Cosmic Ballet of Transformation

The cosmos is a complex mystery, and everything that exists within it follows a cycle of transformation and motion. This is the way of nature, and there is no need to be alarmed.

6. Equity in Collective Purpose

Everything in the world has a purpose and is part of a greater whole. Equity can be found when looking at things in their totality. Do not expect things to be perfect but be willing to accept them for what they are.

7. The Choice is Yours: Which Path Will You Take?

You can make the most of your time and choose wisely.

8. Silence the Courtly Gripes: A Plea

Do not complain about being a courtly life.

9. The Power of Repentance: Embrace or Disregard?

Repentance is a way to become more mindful of the benefits of things and to avoid overlooking them.

10. Unveiling the Mystery: What Lies Beneath?

Think about this complex question: what is this thing in front of us, and why does it exist? Consider its material and how it was created. Investigate its purpose and how long it will last. Examine everything around you.

11. Arousing Change: Nature's Call to Action

Wake up and do something good for others.

12. Exploring the Possibilities: Reason with Yourself

If you have a thought, ask yourself what its nature is, and what qualities it should have.

13. Uncovering Values: Exposing Human Nature

People have opinions about what is good and bad, and they usually act on them.

14. Adjusting Perspective with Wisdom

If you think you know what is best for yourself, be careful not to mistake your opinion for reality. Remember that you are not always right, and that someone else may have a better idea.

15. Empowered to Act: Act or Don't Complain?

You cannot control everything, but you can control your own actions. If you do not like what is happening, take action to change it. Complaining is useless.

16. Universe's Unceasing Transformation: Accept It

At death, everything goes to a new place, and you cannot remove yourself from the universe. Everything will change, but that is okay.

17. The Great Mystery of Life

Everything in the world was created for a reason. You were created for something special too.

18. Nature's End: A Final Consummation

Nature has an end just like everything else does.

19. The Mask of Beauty: Uncovering Life's Vulnerability

Life is short, enjoy the moment and do not worry about the future.

20. Exploring Matter, Dogma, and Meaning

What you need to worry about is the topic itself, not the way it is being presented.

21. A Challenging Choice: Amend Now or Wait?

If you want to be good, today is the day to start.

22. Embracing Difficulties, Trusting Providence

When I act, I trust that it will benefit humanity eventually. Even though I may face difficulties and obstacles, I know that the Gods will guide me to the right path.

23. The Viscous Reality of Life

Daily life is made up of simple tasks, like taking a bath, a mixture of oil, sweat, and dirt that is disgusting and represents the base, unappealing, and loathsome nature of life.

24. The Momentary Journey of Life and Death

Remember that you will one day die and be forgotten.

25. Exploring Human Purpose: A Cosmic Journey

Pursue activities that are in line with who you are as a human being. Consider the source of your actions, the source of the activity, and the people involved.

26. Pain: An Illusion of Evil?

Pain is something that we must all endure, but it does not have to be evil.

27. Unlock Your Divine Potentiality

Remember to use your mind to achieve your goals and be positive!

28. Graceful Humility: The Key to Address All

Speak with dignity and humility, but not with the formal speech of the world.

29. The Last of their Kind: The Pompey Family

Families die, but their memory will live on.

30. Embrace Change; Find Your Path

Keep your focus on your life's one goal and do your best at everything, even if obstacles arise. Embrace change and use it to take a different path that still leads to your life's purpose.

31. Cherish Life's Transience

Do not be too hard on yourself when things go wrong. Remember that life is full of change and that everything will eventually pass away.

32. Reunited: A Journey of Restoration

God values us and has made it possible for us to come together again, even when we are separated from the whole.

33. Turning Adversity into Opportunity

Any obstacle in life can be used to achieve your goals. You can take whatever life throws your way and use it to your advantage.

34. Test Your Resilience: Endure the Present Moment

Do not worry about the future, focus on the present. Everything will be all right.

35. The Pointlessness of Mortality: A Reflection

Mortality is a mystery, and we do not know what will happen in the future.

36. Quick-Sighted Wisdom: Heed His Advice

If you are quick-sighted, be so in matters of judgment and best discretion, he says.

37. Justice vs. Self-Restraint: The Battle of Human Morality

Justice is the most moral quality, but self-restraint is the strongest one.

38. Safety Through Self-Awareness

When we are afraid or upset, it is important to remember that we are not alone. We can use our reason to calm ourselves down, and if we are still feeling scared or upset, we can talk to our feelings to figure out why.

39. Navigating Sensitivity: An Untouchable Mind

Sensitive people can suffer from many ill effects, but with understanding and good habits, they will be fine.

40. Unchanging Certainty

If ever it was round and secure, there is no probability that it will ever alter.

41. Reasoning Rightly: My Path to Bliss

Life is full of ups and downs, but it is important to remember that we all have feelings and should treat others the way we want to be treated.

42. Invest in Your Legacy Now

Think about what you want for yourself and what you wish to leave behind for others. Be yourself and do not let others control how you present yourself to the world.

43. Unconcerned and Content: My Spirit's Journey

Just be yourself, and do not worry about what others think. You will be happy in the end!

44. The Cost of Worth: A Question

Is it worth it to put my soul through such pain, humiliation, chaos, confusion, and fear? What is so valuable that you would go through all of this?

45. Find Peace in the Face of Adversity

Everything happens for a reason, and you can overcome anything if you are patient and kind.

46. Unconquerable Mind: A Fortress of Contentment

Keep your mind focused on what is important, be enthusiastic about what you do, and do not be afraid to defend yourself.

47. Perception is Key: Don't Assume

Listen to what people say, but do not let your own judgement get in the way.

48. The Mysteries of Nature: Transforming the Unprofitable

The universe has a way of transforming old, unprofitable things into something new and useful without having to search outside itself.

49. Vigilance in Virtue: A Path to Wisdom

Be careful not to do anything that will make you unhappy, and always do your best to be virtuous.

50. Sustaining the Fountain of Freedom

To stay strong and pure, you need to strive for the same values in your life.

51. The Pursuit of Approval: A Reflection

You should learn about the world around you and understand its purpose. If you do not, you may not be happy with the things you do, and you may regret it later.

52. Exploring the Intelligent Energy of the Universe

We will continue to share thoughts and ideas with each other, but also the same air, which is everywhere in the universe.

53. Choose Your Own Path: Free from Wrongdoing

Our neighbor's wickedness is only harmful to them and has no effect on us. We can choose our own path and be free from wrongdoing.

54. Aktines of Mind: The Extension of Light

Be yourself, and the sun will shine through.

55. The Comfort of Death: A Reassurance

Death is an inevitability, but it is a natural process that happens to everyone in their own time. It is best to face it head on and not worry about it.

56. One for Another: Unite or Accept?

If someone is not behaving properly, teach them how to behave or tolerate them.

57. Exploring the Labyrinth of the Mind

The mind can wander in many different directions, but it will always get where it is going if you care about it.

58. Exploring the Depths of Minds

To become enlightened, you must journey into the minds of others.

BOOK 9

— Empower with Benevolence

Take a moment for yourself to remember that life is a cycle of joy and sorrow. Follow nature's laws, seek happiness, avoid pain and danger, accept death and uncertainty. Understand the consequences of unjust actions, find contentment in God's will, and clear your mind to align with nature. Be kind and seek happiness, unburden your soul to find peace. Actions matter more than feelings, and being neutral is neither good nor bad. Examine your own feelings to resolve internal conflicts and accept that change is inevitable. Work together for the greater good and seek comfort in spirituality. Embrace the inevitability of choice, self-reflection, life's impermanence, innocence's burden, and the universe's infinite cycle. Choose modesty over vanity, avoid negativity, and free yourself from opinions. When life gets complicated, focus on your intentions, learn humility in an impudent world, and find clarity through prayer.

1. Respecting Nature's Laws: Our Common Cause

People who lie are being impious, as they are rejecting the nature of the universe. Those who pursue pleasure instead of pain are also being impious. Those who dread suffering and misfortune in this world are also being impious.

2. Fleeing from Danger: A Plague of the Mind

Fleeing from danger is the best way to avoid sin.

3. Death: A Part of Natural Life

Remember that death is a natural part of life, and that you will be happy to leave behind those who do not share your beliefs.

4. Consequences of Unjust Acts

If you do something wrong, it is only going to hurt yourself. Being unfair means doing something that harms other people without their permission or consent.

5. Contentment in God's Will

If I do what, I think, is best based on what I know, it is charitable. I am content with whatever comes from God.

6. Clearing the Mind's Clutter

Wiping away fancy means using deliberation and quenching concupiscence means keeping the mind free from distractions.

7. Uniting Nature's Call: A Common Origin

Nature always prevails, and sensible people are drawn to one another.

8. Harvesting Reason: A Multiplication of Nature

Everything in life has a time to come into being. Some things bring forth general benefits, while others produce their own special fruits. Reason is a force of nature that multiplies, creating what it is itself.

9. Empowerment through Benevolence: A Divine Gift

Teach them to be tolerant and grateful for the blessings of the Gods.

10. Seeking Happiness Through Kindness

Remember to act in accordance with the law of charity and communal living, which will lead to happiness and fulfillment.

11. Unburdening My Soul: A Journey to Peace

I overcame my problems today, and now I am happy.

12. The Unchanging Mundanity of Life

Things are the same as they have always been, but they are not always comfortable or pleasant.

13. The Silent Judge: Unvoiced Understanding

It is the understanding that lies without that passes judgement.

14. Actions Speak Louder Than Feelings

People who are kind and helpful are better than those who are angry or hateful. Virtue and wickedness are not judged by how we feel, but by what we do.

15. The Ascendant Stone: No Benefit, No Harm

Things that fall to the ground do not get harmed and things that rise to the top do not benefit.

16. Examining the Examiners: Self-Perception Conflict

Think about what these people represent and why you might be afraid of them.

17. A Flux of Change: Our World Unfolds

Everything is constantly changing and decaying.

18. The Burden of Guilt: Not Yours to Bear

Sin is something that other people do, not you. It is not relevant to you, and it should not bother you.

19. Embracing Life's Endings: A Journey of Transformation

The endings of our lives are just another chapter in our journey, and we should embrace them with detachment and wisdom.

20. Seeking Refuge in Justice: An Exploration of Self and Universe

When you need to, hurry to your own consciousness, the universe, or the one you are currently dealing with. Contemplate if you are in a state of ignorance or knowledge. Remember that the other is kin.

21. Uniting for the Common Good

Always do what is best for the collective, and do not cause division.

22. A Dirge for Children's Anguish

Dead bodies are scary, but anger is insignificant compared to sorrow.

23. Exploring the Impermanence of Causes

By looking at the origin of an outcome, you can understand its limits and how it might change over time.

24. Unsatisfied with Happiness: A Costly Misunderstanding

You could have had a lot of happiness if you would have just embraced it sooner.

25. Unpleasantness? Find Solace in the Gods

Ignore people who try to bring you down, they are probably not worth your time.

26. The Inevitability of Choice: Navigating Life's Cycle

Life is what we make it, and we can always choose to be happy.

27. The Transience of Life: A Reflection

The universe is constantly changing, and everything will eventually be reclaimed by the Earth.

28. Modesty Over Vanity: A Philosophical Call to Action

The wisdom-keepers are important because they know a lot about things. They are also vain and think that they are better than everyone else. But they are wrong, and they should follow their own advice.

29. A Towering View of Life's Complexities

Life is big. Be kind, strive for justice, and accept that fame and honor are fleeting.

30. Free Yourself from Opinion: Discover More Space

You cannot change the world, but you can change your own life. So, use your power to make the world a better place.

31. Exploring the Transience of Life

Life is a never-ending cycle of change and chaos, with nothing truly permanent. Beyond life and death lies an eternity of existence.

32. The Human Condition: Revealed

Observe their minds, wisdom, and passions. Learn their values and aversions. Envision their exposed souls. They feel the sting of unjust criticism and bask in praise for virtuous deeds. Their vanity and conceit are abundant.

33. The Universe's Unending Cycle: Is There Hope?

Life goes on and things will change, but that does not mean that everything is bad. In fact, it is probably just a part of the natural order.

34. Life: A Paradox of Lowly and Regal

It is a paradox that substances as humble as water, dust, and the mixture of bones in our bodies can be infected, while highly admired objects like marble, gold, silver, and even the realest apparel are made from ordinary materials like sheep hair and shellfish blood. Life is no exception, as it is just a fleeting breath of ever-changing blood that shares the same fate as everything else.

35. Uncovering the Unexpected: Grumbling, Moaning and Deceit

Do your best to have a good relationship with your siblings, and do not worry so much about what they are saying.

36. A Century of Change in Three Years

The future is what we make of it.

37. The Burden of Innocence: His Fate in My Hands

Do not blame yourself if something bad happens. It may not have been your fault.

38. The Grand Scheme Unfolds: Accepting Our Fate

Everything happens for a reason. Even death is a part of life, and it is important to remember that.

39. The Immortal Soul's Mortality?

The rational part of your brain is just like other animals and is subject to death.

40. Unlock Your Mind with Prayer

Prayer is a way to focus on the things we can control and improve our lives.

41. Epicurus' Remedy for Adversity: A Philosophical Perspective

Keep your spirits high even when things get tough, and do not be swayed by the opinions of others.

42. Mind Your Craft: Focus and Intent

Professionals always try to focus on what they are doing and the tools they are using right now.

43. Learning Meekness in a World of Impudence

When dealing with people who are impudent, be gentle and consider what virtues nature has given us to counter such vices.

BOOK 10

— Unveiling Your Inner Strength

Take charge of your life and appreciate its beauty. Follow your heart and ignore unimportant things. It is fine to make mistakes; you do not have to be perfect to be a good person. Remember that everything in the world is connected, so consider the well-being of others. Everything changes with time, so aim to be kind, humble, and honest. Doubt and fear can bring success or failure, so persist even when you fail. A good person is honest, polite, and helpful; focus on those qualities. Your beliefs and actions are all that matter. Nature provides food and water for everyone's benefit, and the world loves everything. Embrace life as a journey and make the most of it, as it is a mystery, and we cannot control everything.

1. The Joy of Spiritual Freedom

Your spirit will be unadulterated and absolute, more visible, and transparent than the body that contains you. You will experience the joy of those who seek love and whose souls are not weighed down by material things. You will be complete and require nothing from the cosmos, no delight from living or the inanimate. You will be content in the present and all that encompasses you, believing that all is ordained by the divine for your ultimate wellbeing, bliss, and life. You will embrace the holy, and among mankind, your comportment will be such that you will never complain nor do anything to justifiably be condemned.

2. Living with Nature's Guidance

Follow your nature, and do not be distracted by trivialities.

3. Be Ready for Anything: Embrace the Challenge

Do not be afraid to take on whatever comes your way, even if it is tough. You are tough, and you can handle it.

4. Compassionate Education: A Path to Redemption

It is okay to be wrong, and you do not have to be perfect to be a good person.

5. Fate's Unfinished Tapestry

You are not in control, but that does not mean you cannot make the most of your life.

6. Unlock Cosmic Happiness: Share the Good of the Whole

Remember that everything in the natural world is interconnected, and you should always think of the well-being of others. You will be a happy, content citizen of any city.

7. Time's Unwavering Alterations: Nature's Intention or Mistake?

Everything in the world will eventually change, and this is a natural process. Everything in the world is composed of different elements, and when these elements are broken down, they return to the generative seeds of the universe.

8. Behold the Power of Being Good, Modest, and True!

Take on the qualities of attentiveness, contentment, and expansiveness (ἔμφρων, σύμφρων, and ὑπέρφρων), and to never dishonor these traits. By embodying these values, we can start a new life full of joy. If we slip back into old habits, we should find a quiet place or accept death willingly instead of succumbing to rage. We should remember that the gods expect us to function as rational creatures and live up to these values, just as other creatures live naturally to their characteristics.

9. Unearth True Simplicity: Revelation in Action & Contemplation

Toys and games are just means to an end. We must use them to learn and grow, and to enjoy life more fully.

10. The Hunter's Pursuit: Seeking New Prey

Arachnids, hunters, and warriors all chase after their next meal to feel happy and proud.

11. Revel in the Rhythm of Change

To be successful in life, you need to be persistent and learn from your failures.

12. Liberated by Faith: His Final Journey

A person died and went to heaven. He was happy there and was content with what God had in store for him.

13. Pursuing True Happiness: Seek Wise Counsel

Doubt and apprehension can lead to success or failure, but it is important to weigh the pros and cons before making a decision.

14. The Rational Fool: A Paradox

What is it that moves at a sluggish pace, yet is swift? Cheerful, yet solemn? He that in all matters adheres to rationality as his guide.

15. The Morning Question: Dare You Take the Reins?

The only things that matter in life are what you believe and what you do.

16. Surrendering to Love's Delight

The wise person is humble and allows others to give them what they want.

17. Living True in a World of Indifference

Live as if you were apart from society and let them observe a human being that is truly living in accordance with his nature.

18. Be a Good Man: A Challenge

A good man is honest, polite, and helpful.

19. From Speck to Oblivion: The Impermanence of Life

Think about how immense everything that has existed, exists, and will exist truly is. Every particle is tiny compared to the big picture. Reflect on everything you come across in life, envisioning its inevitable decline, deterioration, and disappearance − becoming a mere memory in the blink of an eye.

20. Futility of Life: A Moment of Reflection

Life is a never-ending journey, full of highs and lows.

21. Nature's Gift to All

When nature provides things like food and water, everyone benefits.

22. Loving What Once Was: A World Full of Wonder

The world loves everything that exists and what once was.

23. Life is Yours to Journey: Find Courage and Comfort!

The choices you make in life will determine your destiny. Whether you retire or continue living, make the most of your journey.

24. Exploring Loneliness: Plato's Questions

Living a solitary life is not as bad as you might think. You can find happiness and fulfillment in the company of others, even on the most solitary of mountaintops.

25. Runaways of the Universe: A Universal Truth

To be a fugitive, you must abandon the law.

26. Witnessing Life's Miraculous Journey

Life is a mystery, and we cannot always control what happens. But we can watch it happen and learn from it.

27. The Timelessness of Humanity

All things happen for a reason, and everything turns out okay in the end.

28. Cries of Mortality: Accepting Providence's Will

Life is full of pain and sorrow, but it is also a journey towards enlightenment.

29. Life's Last Reflection: Regretful Realization?

Make a list of things you will not do again once you die.

30. Forgiveness During Transgression

When someone affronts you, try to reflect on why they may have done it and how you can forgive them. If you can, try to take away the thing that made them do it in the first place.

31. A Glimpse of Eternity: Where Are They Now?

Meditate on the great philosophers and thinkers of history and imagine how their ideas have influenced your life. Remember that their ideas will change and progress over time, so do not be afraid to experiment with new things.

32. Unlock the Splendors of Understanding

Stay patient and learn everything you can about life. It is an opportunity to understand things in all their truth.

33. Be Natural, Be Free: A Citizen's Right

Be yourself and do not try to be someone you are not.

34. Leaves in the Wind: A Reflection on Mortality

Life is a cycle of growth and decay.

35. Indifference: The Key to Contentment

You need to have good eyesight, good hearing, and a good sense of smell to be able to survive in the world. You should also try to be liked by your children and by other people.

36. The Inevitable Parting: Nature's Way

Death is natural and inevitable but be kind to those around you when you leave this world.

37. Unlock the Power of Self-Reflection

Ask yourself why you are doing what you are doing and what the consequences will be.

38. Unlock Your Rhetoric Power: Man Himself

The body is nothing without the power of the inner cause.

BOOK 11

— The Journey of Self-Discovery

Act now and show kindness to those around you. Appreciate art and nature, find balance between knowledge and experience, connect with others, be true to yourself, do what brings you joy, embrace emotions, follow cosmic order, collaborate, confront fears, remember history, be wise and articulate, learn something new, be patient and humble, accept life's cycle of transformation and progress.

1. Reasonable Souls and Natural Privileges: One and the Same

The prerogatives and privileges of a rational soul are manifold, including the ability to see itself, to arrange and organize itself, to craft itself however it wishes, to reap the rewards of its actions, and to make sure that whatever it has in hand is made complete and full.

2. Don't Be Fooled by the Whole: Dissect the Details

When considering what you admire, always remember to dissect the details, and you will eventually arrive at contempt for the whole spectacle.

3. Ready for Eternity: A Discreet Conviction

Souls that are prepared for separation from the body are happy and content.

4. Achieving Goodness: Exploring Nature's Laws

You can achieve your purpose in life by understanding the laws and principles of nature.

5. Life's Wisdom Through Tragedy and Comedy

Tragedy is a reminder of our fleeting existence, and the consequences of our actions. It teaches us to be humble and to enjoy life.

6. The Philosopher's Dilemma: Knowledge or Experience?

A philosopher's life can be a balance between knowledge and experience.

7. Rejoining the Garden: Bridging the Gap of Separation

We are all related to each other, and it is important to reunite with our neighbors.

8. Unite in Love, Not Opinion: Embrace Courage, Not Fear

Be kind, and do not let fear stop you from doing what is right. Stay united with your friends and loved ones, no matter what.

9. Nature's Justice: Imitating the Unbeatable

Art is the weakest force in the world, but it makes something better from something worse, which is the basis of justice.

10. The Pursuit of Stillness

Do not worry about the things you want; they will still be there when you are done chasing them.

11. Illuminating the Soul's True Essence

The soul is like a perfect globe that is undistorted and has a brilliant light shining on it.

12. The Phocion Way: Unshakable Resilience

I will not be contemptible, hateful, or impatient. I will be kind and loving, and that is all that matters.

13. Competition of Egos: A Descent into Vanity

The people who are most successful in life are usually the ones who are most humble.

14. Concealing Goodness: A Mask of Deceit?

People who pretend to be good are just not honest. They are not good at all.

15. Seeking Inner Joy: A Quest for Happiness

Be yourself, do what makes you happy, and do not let anyone stop you from achieving your dreams.

16. Navigating Life's Complications: Meekness is Key

Anger and grief are natural consequences of wrongdoing, but they are not always a dreadful thing.

17. Unleash Your Higher Self: Mindful Transformation

There are four inclinations of the mind: to think, to feel, to will, and to enjoy. Whenever you recognize them, you should correct them. Say to yourself, "This thought is not necessary," "This is uncharitable," "I will speak as another man's slave or instrument," and "Nothing can be more senseless and absurd.".

18. The Universal Call for Order: Obey!

You are made up of all the elements, and you must obey the cosmic order. Even the elements must obey the universe, and they will stay in their places until they are dismissed.

19. Living with Collective Purpose: The Key to Consistency

Achieving a common, communal goal is a clever way to stay consistent throughout your life.

20. The Fear of Country Mice: A Tale

The country mouse and the city mouse lived in distinct parts of the world, and they each had a lot of fun doing their own thing. But one day, the city mouse came to visit the country mouse and saw all the food and things in the country mouse's home. The city mouse was so scared that she ran away as fast as she could.

21. Concerns of the World: Socrates' Warning

Socrates said that the appropriate fear of the world is silly children's fears.

22. Shadow Seats for Strangers: The Lacedæmonians' Generosity

The Lacedæmonians typically provided seating and benches for their visitors in the shade at their public spectacles, while they were content to sit anywhere.

23. The Fatal Cost of Gratitude: Socrates' Refusal

Socrates said that he feared the worst kind of death — the death of not being able to repay the kindness bestowed upon him.

24. Honoring Ancient Wisdom: An Ephesian Tale

Remembering people from the past who have done remarkable things is important so that we can learn from them and be inspired to do even more things ourselves.

25. A Cosmic Duty: Revealing the Unadorned Beauty of the Heavens

The Pythagoreans were constantly looking up at the sky and were reminded of the cosmic order and duty of those who followed their path.

26. The Brilliant Nudity of Socrates

Socrates, a famous philosopher known for his intelligence and humor, faced a dilemma when his wife Xanthippe took away his clothes. He appeared in front of his peers wearing only a skin, causing them to feel surprised and embarrassed. Despite this, Socrates made a joke, advising his friends not to look directly at him as his naked body was too glorious to manage.

27. Unlock the Mystery of Life: Experience It!

Education is the key to unlocking the mysteries of life.

28. Virtue Under Fire

Even though people will accuse others of being evil, virtuous people will still be shamed.

29. Longing in Vain: The Childless Dream

Those who long for figs in the winter, when they cannot be obtained, are like those who long for children before they are granted.

30. Life's Eternal Transformation: A Father's Whisper

Life is a cycle of change and growth, and nothing is ever utterly lost.

31. The Wisdom of Choice: What Path Do We Take?

The free will is important to keep in mind, as it can help us be more considerate and respectful of others.

BOOK 12

— Embrace Life and Find Balance

Life is short and unpredictable, so it is important to take time to appreciate the good things and focus on what is important. Let us aim high, be honest, and remain in control of our own lives. Death is inevitable, so let us seize every opportunity for happiness in life. It is important to strive for balance and justice, and to recognize the presence of the divine in everyday life. Remember that everything is interconnected, and it all depends on your point of view. Life is brief, so make the most of it and constantly reflect on your true purpose while taking actions for the greater good.

1. Unlock Your True Nature: Live with Courage and Clarity

Aspire to greatness, trust in the gods, speak honestly, do the right thing, and do not let anyone else's words, or your own basic needs, impede you.

2. Living a Life of Clarity: Detach and Be Ready to Depart

To be like God, rid yourself of the unnecessary encumbrance of the body, life, and material possessions. Focus instead on the third and only thing that is truly yours – your mind. Detach from it all external entanglements, from others' deeds and words to troublesome thoughts of the future, and the vagaries of life. Make your mind like a sphere, continually ready to depart, just, accepting, and speaking the truth.

3. The Weight of Judgment: Our Own vs Others

We care more about what others think of us than what we think of ourselves.

4. The Gods' Perfect Creation: Unjustified Immortality

The universe is perfect and good, and we can trust that the Gods did not overlook anything when they made it.

5. Left-Handed Strength: Embracing the Impossible

Sometimes the things that seem impossible may actually be the best thing for us.

6. Wrestling with Beliefs: A Pancratiast's Approach

Death is inevitable, and it is natural to be scared. But remember that life is short and that everything passes away eventually. You should focus on the things that matter most and live your life to the fullest.

7. Contemplating the World: Matter, Form, and End

Form is what a thing looks like, and matter is what it is made of. Reference is what something refers to. Matter and form can change, but reference always stays the same.

8. The Divine Gift of Contentment

Being human is a great gift, and we should all strive to receive contentment in all that is sent to us.

9. Innocence of Ignorance: No Blame

No one is to blame for any sad things that happen, even if they are not aware of what is going on or if they are deliberately doing bad things.

10. Life's Oddities: A Puzzling Paradox

Sometimes things happen that do not make sense, but they are just part of the natural cycle of life.

11. Unraveling Fate: The Journey of Self-Determination

The world is a chaotic and unpredictable place, but we can still make ourselves happy and successful.

12. Can We Really Condemn Others for Their "Sins"?

Sometimes people do things that we do not like, but we cannot change. Sometimes we feel like we need to make a judgment, but it is not always easy to know what to do.

13. The Art of Self-Determination

If you do not feel comfortable or obligated to do something, do not do it.

14. Unveiling the True Nature: A Journey of Discovery

Observe what is around you and try to understand its purpose and how long it will last.

15. Unlock Your True Purpose: Beyond Body & Mind

Ask yourself what your true purpose is, and make sure that what you do is for the good of all. Time moves swiftly, so make the most of your life while you can.

16. The Calm of Perception

If you can remove your own thoughts and views, you can see the world in a more peaceful and secure way.

17. The Divinely Led and Inspired: A Pause of Nature's Design

He stopped doing what he did because he did not want to do it anymore — it was not bad for him, and he was not harmed.

18. Ready for the Ultimate Test?

Remember to be respectful of nature and the divine and be prepared for the end of the world.

19. Abandon Notions: What Stops You?

Abandon your notions of who you are, what you should do, and what is best for you, and you will be safe.

20. The Impermanence of Power and Fortune

People achieve wonderful things, suffer great losses, and eventually die. These events are transient and insignificant in the grand scheme of things. We should embrace moderation and justice and remember that we all face the same fate.

21. Believing in the Unseen: My Devotion to the Gods

I believe in the Gods because they are seen in action every day and I hold my own soul in high esteem.

22. Unlock the Path to Virtue: Truth and Justice

The key to living a good life is mastering the truths of the world. We should strive for justice and honesty, and consistently do virtuous deeds without interruption if we desire.

23. Unity Amidst Division: An Uninterrupted Bond

Everything in the world is one, and though it is divided, it is just a matter of perspective. Just as one's own mind is one, so too is the world one.

24. The Choice of Life: Think Carefully

Think carefully about whether you want to live forever. Remember, God and reason will guide you in the end.

25. A Moment in Infinity: Our Place in Time

Life is short, enjoy it while you can.

26. Answer Unknown: Searching for Clarity

The extent of my understanding is unknown, while everything else beyond my control is meaningless and insignificant, like a puff of smoke.

27. Farewell with Joy: The Duty of He Who Dismisses

To help someone accept death, many things can be powerful, even for those who value pleasure and fear discomfort. Death may not be scary for someone who only thinks about what is expected in life. What matters is doing good, whether we do many or few good things.

Whether the world lasts a long time or a brief time, it is not relevant. We all live in this big city of the world as citizens, no matter how long we are here. We have lived if we were meant to, which is comforting. So, why be upset when it is nature, not an unfair judge or a tyrant, which is sending us away?

It is like a director ending an actor's role in a play. The play is not over yet. You are right, in life there are only three acts. It is up to the one who made us to decide when our part ends. It is not our concern. So, let us go with joy and contentment because the one dismissing us feels the same way.

GLOSSARY

This Glossary includes all proper names (excepting a few which are insignificant or unknown) and all obsolete or obscure words.

Adrianus, or Hadrian (76–138 A.D.), 14th Roman Emperor.

Agrippa, M. Vipsanius (63–12 B.C.), a distinguished soldier under Augustus.

Alexander the Great, King of Macedonia, and Conqueror of the East, 356–323 B.C.

Antisthenes of Athens, Cynic founder, and Plato foe, lived in the fifth century BC. Antoninus Pius, meanwhile, was the 15th Roman Emperor from 138 to 161 A.D. and one of the finest rulers to ever don a crown.

Apathia, the Stoic ideal was calmness in all circumstances, an insensibility to pain, and absence of all exaltation at, pleasure or good fortune.

Apelles, a renowned painter of antiquity.

Apollonius of Alexandria, called Dyscolus, or the "ill-tempered," a great grammarian.

Aposteme, tumor, excrescence.

Archimedes of Syracuse, 287–212 B.C., the most famous mathematician of antiquity.

Athos, a mountain promontory at the N. of the Aegean Sea.

Augustus, first Roman Emperor (ruled 31 B.C.–14 A.D.).

Avoid, void.

Bacchius: there were several persons of this name, and the one meant is the musician.

Brutus (1) the liberator of the Roman people from their kings, and (2) the murderer of Cæsar. Both names were household words.

Cæsar, Caius, Julius, the Dictator and Conqueror.

Caieta, a town in Latium.

Camillus, a famous dictator in the early days of the Roman Republic.

Carnuntum, a town on the Danube in Upper Pannonia.

Cato, called of Utica, a Stoic who died by his own hand after the battle of Thapsus, 46 B.C. His name was proverbial for virtue and courage.

Cautelous, cautious.

Cecrops, first legendary King of Athens.

Charax, the priestly historian of that name, whose date is unknown, except that it must be later than Nero.

Chirurgeon, surgeon.

Chrysippus, 280–207 B.C., a Stoic philosopher, and the founder of Stoicism as a systematic philosophy.

The Circus Maximus of Rome, a place of entertainment, where four Factiones, or companies, vied for supremacy. Each one distinguished by its own color: red, white, blue, and green. Though the competition was fierce, with many outbreaks of violence, it was a place of joy and celebration. Where laughter and applause echoed through the stands, and champions were made, and rivalries were formed. A place of great spectacle, and an arena of immense rivalry.

Cithaeron, a mountain range N. of Attica.

Comedy, ancient; a term applied to the Attic comedy of Aristophanes and his time, which criticized persons and politics, like a modern comic journal, such as Punck. See New Comedy.

Compendious, short.

Conceit, opinion.

Contentation, contentment.

Crates, a Cynic philosopher of the fourth century B.C.

Crœsus, King of Lydia, proverbial for wealth; he reigned 560-546 B.C.

The Cynics, a school of philosophers led by Antisthenes, sought a return to a state of nature by rejecting all civil and social claims. Their texts were a tongue-in-cheek version of Socraticism, where virtue alone was seen as good and vice as bad. Though their mission was noble, their manners were often unpleasant – a contradiction that is still manifest in society today.

Demetrius of Phalerum, an Athenian orator, statesman, philosopher, and poet. Born 345 B.C.

Democritus of Abdera (460-361 B.C.), celebrated as the "laughing philosopher", whose constant thought was "What fools these mortals be." He invented the Atomic Theory.

Dio of Syracuse, a disciple of Plato, and afterward tyrant of Syracuse. Murdered 353 B.C.

Diogenes, the Cynic, born about 412 B.C., renowned for his rudeness and hardihood.

Diognetus, a painter.

Dispense with, put up with.

Dogmata, pithy sayings, or philosophical rules of life.

Empedocles of Agrigentum, fl. 5th century B.C., a philosopher, who first laid down that there were "four elements". He believed in the transmigration of souls, and the indestructibility of matter.

Epictetus, a renowned Stoic philosopher, was of Phrygian origin. He started as a slave and later became a freedman, yet remained lame, impoverished, and nonetheless content. His discourses were subsequently collected and published in the work known as the Encheiridion, compiled by one of his pupils.

Epicureans, a sect of philosophers founded by Epicurus, who "combined the physics of Democritus," i.e., the atomic theory, "with the ethics of Aristippus." They proposed to live for happiness, but the word did not bear that coarse and vulgar sense originally which it soon took.

Epicurus of Samos, 342-270 B.C. At Athens, in his verdant gardens, he led a life of urbanity and benevolence, albeit unproductive. His character was uncomplicated and temperate, and possessed none of the vices or excesses that would later be attributed to the Epicurean school.

Eudoxus of Cnidus, a famous astronomer and physician of the fourth century B. C.

Fatal, fated.

Fortuit, chance (adj.).

Fronto, M. Cornelius, a rhetorician and pleader, made consul in 143 A.D. Several of his letters to M, Aur. and others are extant.

Granua, a tributary of the Danube.

Helice, the ancient capital city of Achaia, swallowed up by an earthquake, 373 B.C.

Helvidius Priscus, son-in-law of Thrasea Paetus, a noble man and a lover of liberty. He was banished by Nero and put to death by Vespasian.

Heraclitus of Ephesus, who lived in the sixth century B.C. He wrote on philosophy and natural science.

Herculaneum, near Mount Vesuvius, buried by the eruption of 79 A.D.

Hiatus, gap.

Hipparchus of Bithynia, an astronomer of the second century B.C., "The true father of astronomy."

Hippocrates of Cos, about 460-357 B.C. One of the most well-known physicians of antiquity.

Idiot, means merely the non-proficient in anything, the "layman," he who was not technically trained in any art, craft, or calling.

Leonnatus, a distinguished general under Alexander the Great.

Lucilla, daughter of M. Aurelius, and wife of Verus, whom she survived.

Mæcenas, a trusted adviser of Augustus, and a munificent patron of wits and literary men.

Maximus, Claudius, a Stoic philosopher.

Menippus, a Cynic philosopher.

Meteores, ta metewrologika, "high philosophy," used specially of astronomy and natural philosophy, which were bound up with other speculations.

Middle Comedy, something midway between the Old and New Comedy. See Comedy, Ancient, and New Comedy.

The Stoics distinguished between three realms: the virtuous, the vicious, and the "indifferent." Yet, much of what the world views as either good or bad, such as wealth or poverty, they view as "indifferent." Of such matters, some were to be pursued, while others were to be rejected.

Muses, the nine deities who presided over various kinds of poesy, music, etc. Their leader was Apollo, one of whose titles is Musegetes, the Leader of the Muses.

Nerves, strings.

New Comedy, the Attic Comedy of Menander, and his school, which criticized not persons but manners, like a modern comic opera. See Comedy, Ancient.

Palestra, wrestling school.

Pancratiast, competitor in the pancratium, a combined contest which comprises boxing and wrestling.

Parmularii, gladiators armed with a small round shield (parma).

Pheidias, the most famous sculptor of antiquity.

Philippus, founder of the Macedonian supremacy, and father of Alexander the Great.

Phocion, an Athenian general and statesman, a noble and high-minded man, fourth century B.C., Demosthenes called him, "the pruner of my periods." He was put to death by the State in 317, on a false suspicion, and left a message for his son "to bear no grudge against the Athenians".

Pine, torment.

Plato of Athens, 429-347 B.C. He used the dialectic method invented by his master Socrates. He was a philosopher-poet, they say, whose Theory of Ideas stated that things were what they were based on their participation in the eternal Idea. He envisioned a Utopian world in his "Commonwealth," a place of perfection and harmony.

Platonics, followers of Plato.

Pompeii, near Mount Vesuvius, buried in the eruption of 79 A.D.

Pompeius, C. Pompeius Magnus, an extraordinarily successful general at the end of the Roman Republic (106-48 B.C.).

Prestidigitator, juggler.

Pythagoras of Samos, a philosopher, scientist, and moralist of the sixth century B.C.

Quadi, a tribe of S. Germany. M. Aurelius continued war against them, and part of this book was written in the field.

Rictus, gape, jaws.

Rusticus, Q. Junius, or Stoic philosopher, twice made consul by M. Aurelius.

Sacrary, shrine.

Salaminius, Leon of Salamis. The Thirty Tyrants ordered Socrates to fetch him before them, and Socrates, at his own peril, refused.

Sarmatae, a tribe dwelling in Poland.

Sceletum, skeleton.

The profound musings of Pyrrho, an ancient Greek philosopher who lived four centuries before the birth of Christ, have long been a source of contemplation and inquiry. His teachings on the relativity of knowledge and the impossibility of proof have inspired a school of thought known as "scepticism." His words, though uttered millennia ago, remain as relevant today as they were in his native land. Agnosticism, too, shares many of Pyrrho's philosophical principles, making the two schools of thought natural companions in the pursuit of knowledge.

Scipio, the name of two great soldiers, P. Corn. Scipio Africanus, conqueror of Hannibal, and P.

Corn. Sc. Afr. Minor, who came into the family by adoption, who destroyed Carthage.

Secutoriani (a word coined by C.), the Sececutores, light-armed gladiators, who were pitted against others with net and trident.

Sextus of Chaeronea, a Stoic philosopher, nephew of Plutarch.

Silly, simple, common.

Sinuessa, a town in Latium.

Socrates, an Athenian philosopher (469-399 B.C.), founder of the dialectic method. Put to death on a trumped-up charge by his countrymen.

Stint, limit (without implying niggardliness).

The Stoic way of life was founded by a wise man named Zeno in the fourth century B.C. and was later systematized by Chrysippus in the third century. They believed physical matter was the essence of the universe, and their goal was to live in accordance with nature. Their perfect man had no wants; all he needed was his own wisdom. Virtue was prized, and vice was frowned upon, although they believed external things were of no consequence.

Theophrastus, a philosopher, pupil of Aristotle, and his successor as president of the Lyceum. He wrote many works on philosophy and natural history. Died 287 B.C.

Thrasea, P. Thrasea Pactus, a senator and Stoic philosopher, a noble and courageous man. He was condemned to death by Nero.

Tiberius, 2nd Roman Emperor (14-31 A.D.). He spent the latter part of his life at Capreae (Capri), off Naples, in luxury or debauchery, neglecting his imperial duties.

To-torn, torn to pieces.

Trajan, 13th Roman Emperor, 52-117 A.D.

Verus, Lucius Aurelius, colleague of M. Aurelius in the Empire. He married Lucilla, daughter of M. A., and died in 169 A.D.

Vespasian, 9th Roman Emperor Xenocrates of Chalcedon, 396-314 B.C., a philosopher, and president of the Academy.

INDEX

a good person, 1, 7, 63, 64
a part of, 14, 42, 43, 47, 61, 62
a puff of, 78
a sense of, 15
Abdera, 83
ability, 7, 17, 22, 33
absence, 81
accordance, 58, 66, 87
accordance with nature, 87
accordance with the, 58
accuse, 73
action, 49, 78
actions, 7, 8, 13, 23, 30, 41, 42, 43,
    45, 49, 51, 52, 57, 63, 69, 70, 75
activities, 2, 52
Adrianus, 81
advantage, 53
advice, 18, 60
affections, 42
Agrigentum, 83
Agrippa, 81
albeit, 7, 84
Alexander, 10, 11, 81, 84, 85
Alexandria, 81
all of us, 30
all the same, 24
and make the, 23, 25, 49, 63
and make the most, 23, 25, 49, 63
and not to, 5
and you will be, 14, 18, 25, 31, 39,
    41, 42, 45, 78

anger and passion, 1
anticipation, 29
antiquity, 81, 84, 85
Antisthenes, 81, 83
anyone, 22, 30, 71, 75
Apathia, 81
Apelles, 81
Apollonius, 10, 81
Aposteme, 81
apparel, 61
applause, 82
appreciation, 33
Archimedes, 81
areas, 4, 46
arise, 53
arises, 30
armholes, 30
as if it were, 14
assist, 3
Athens, 4, 81, 82, 84, 85
Athos, 81
attach, 30
attention, 22, 44
Augustus, 81, 84
authority, 30
avoid, 1, 9, 13, 14, 15, 50, 57, 58
Avoid, 18, 49, 81
Bacchius, 82
balance, 9, 69, 70, 75
barbarians, 2
barrier, 30

battle, 2, 7, 82
be content with, 38
be distracted by, 64
be kind and, 70
begin, 25
believe, 6, 8, 27, 28, 29, 65, 78
benefits, 9, 18, 50, 58, 66
benevolence, 12, 33, 84
benevolent, 19
Bithynia, 84
blessings, 58
blood, 23, 61
bodies, 37, 44, 60, 61
bones, 61
books, 4, 5, 19
break, 22
breath, 30, 61
brightness, 36
brother, 11
brothers, 12
Brutus, 82
burden, 57
but they are, 59, 71, 77
Cæsar, 82
Caieta, 82
calmness, 81
Camillus, 82
can be found, 50
capacity, 29, 30
career, 24
Carnuntum, 82
carvings, 2
Cato, 82
cause, 12, 25, 60, 68
Cautelous, 82
Cecrops, 82
centuries, 8, 86
Chaeronea, 87
challenge, 39, 45
challenges, 5, 21, 26, 33, 36
champions, 82
chance, 6, 13, 84
changes, 14, 29, 63
chaos, 24, 54, 61
Charax, 82
charge, 13, 17, 27, 63, 87
charity, 58

children, 3, 11, 24, 68, 73
Chirurgeon, 82
choices, 2, 17, 66
Chrysippus, 4, 82, 87
circumstances, 37, 81
Circus, 82
Cithaeron, 82
citizens, 79
claims, 36, 83
clarity, 13, 57
Cnidus, 84
come together, 53
comedy, 82
Comedy, 82, 85
comfort, 3, 5, 27, 41, 57, 59, 77
comforts, 36
comments, 5
commitment, 36
community, 5, 6, 29, 42
companions, 86
company, 66
compassion, 6, 9, 33
compassionate, 6
Compendious, 82
complain, 50, 64
composure, 28, 34
Conceit, 82
concern, 6, 37, 79
concupiscence, 58
conflict, 18
confusion, 54
connection, 18
consequence, 87
consequences, 57, 68, 70, 71
constitution, 35
contemplation, 86
contempt, 69
Contentation, 82
contributions, 4
control, 5, 25, 27, 28, 29, 30, 33,
        34, 37, 42, 44, 49, 51, 54, 62,
        63, 64, 67, 75, 78
cooperate, 4
cornfield, 44
corruption, 7
Cos, 84
cosmos, 42, 50, 63

country, 71
courage, 6, 82
craft, 24, 37, 69, 84
Crates, 82
creator, 23
creatures, 42, 65
criminals, 37
criticism, 44, 61
Crœsus, 83
cycle, 28, 38, 43, 44, 50, 57, 61, 67, 69, 73, 77
cycle of life, 43, 77
damage, 28
danger, 57, 58
daughter, 1, 2, 84, 87
death, 7, 13, 23, 26, 28, 29, 38, 43, 44, 51, 57, 58, 62, 64, 72, 79, 84, 85, 87
debauchery, 87
decay, 67
deception, 17
decision, 65
decisions, 18, 22, 23
degree, 10, 31
deities, 4, 85
deity, 23
deliberation, 58
delicacy, 10
Demetrius, 83
Democritus, 83
desire, 78
despair, 44
despot, 10
details, 19, 69
deterioration, 66
determination, 11, 30
difference, 13
difficulties, 52
dignity, 52
Dio, 83
Diogenes, 83
Diognetus, 10, 83
directions, 56
discretion, 53
doctors, 28
Dogmata, 83
drawn, 58

duties, 5, 87
education, 2
effect, 25, 55
efforts, 28
elements, 36, 64, 71, 83
emotions, 3, 6, 14, 19, 38, 39, 69
Empedocles, 83
emperor, 3, 5, 7
emperors, 1
encumbrance, 75
endings, 59
endure, 52
ensure, 39
entanglements, 75
entertainment, 82
entities, 30
environment, 17, 33, 34
Ephesus, 84
Epictetus, 83
Epicureans, 3, 83
Epicurus, 83, 84
essence, 29, 87
esteem, 78
eternity, 61
ethics, 83
Eudoxus, 84
even if it, 28, 38, 44, 64
even if they, 38, 76
events, 14, 38, 42, 78
everyone, 2, 5, 26, 29, 38, 42, 45, 56, 60, 66
excellence, 41, 45
exceptions, 30
existence, 13, 33, 61, 70
expectations, 19
experience, 14, 22, 63, 69, 70
experiences, 4
faculties, 29
faculty, 46
family, 1, 6, 11, 86
Fatal, 84
father, 9, 11, 84, 85
fault, 62
fears, 69, 72
feelings, 5, 6, 18, 41, 54, 57
feels, 7, 79
floods, 2

followers, 3, 86
for those who, 79
force, 4, 25, 30, 58, 70
forces, 2
foresaw, 8
forms, 4, 29
fortitude, 18
Fortuit, 84
fortune, 11, 32, 81
freedom, 3, 28
friends, 10, 11, 36, 70, 72
from the path, 23
Fronto, 84
generations, 35
generosity, 6, 11
globe, 70
go ahead, 28
goals, 21, 23, 31, 46, 52, 53
good man, 66
goodness, 6
governs, 6
graciousness, 36
grammar, 10
grandeur, 8
Granua, 84
ground, 59
group, 1, 9
happens to you, 29
happiness, 5, 6, 8, 19, 26, 32, 57,
    58, 60, 66, 75, 83
harmony, 25, 86
harms, 58
health, 2, 5, 28
heart, 1, 5, 6, 14, 18, 63
Helice, 84
Helvidius, 84
Heraclitus, 84
Herculaneum, 84
Hiatus, 84
Hipparchus, 84
Hippocrates, 84
history, 67, 69, 87
hoard, 25
homeland, 38
honest, 7, 18, 46, 63, 66, 71, 75
honesty, 17, 78
honors, 35

human nature, 28
humanity, 9, 49, 52
humans, 4, 24, 30
humility, 6, 36, 52, 57
ideals, 6
ideas, 4, 5, 7, 18, 34, 55, 67
Idiot, 84
if you are, 54, 60
if you do, 46
ignore, 30, 63
illness, 3, 28
impact, 9, 27, 33, 49
importance, 5, 25
in accordance with nature, 4
in all things, 21
in harmony with, 4, 5
in the blink, 66
in the blink of, 66
in the face, 5
in the face of, 5
in the gods, 75
in the grand, 6, 78
in the grand scheme, 6, 78
in the world, 17, 36, 37, 39, 43, 50,
    51, 63, 64, 68, 70, 78
in this life, 6, 35
inclinations, 71
incorrect, 10
inevitability, 56, 57
influence, 7
inform, 10
inner, 5, 9, 13, 14, 18, 68
insight, 31
integrity, 11, 17
intelligence, 72
intention, 33
intentions, 7, 8, 37, 57
interest, 49
interests, 39
is best for, 18, 38, 39, 51, 60, 78
is for the, 77
is not a, 11, 28, 31, 66, 77
is part of, 50
is the way, 50
is to be, 4, 5
journey, 3, 5, 19, 39, 56, 59, 63,
    66, 67

judgment, 53, 77
justice, 9, 23, 61, 70, 75, 78
kinds, 85
kings, 82
lasts, 44, 79
leader, 2, 3, 85
legacy, 7
Leonnatus, 84
letters, 10, 36, 84
life and death, 61
life throws at, 34, 45
life will be, 19
limit, 21, 87
limits, 60
linger, 23
losses, 78
Lucilla, 84, 87
luxury, 87
Mæcenas, 84
make wise, 17, 23
manage, 31, 72
many things, 11, 79
marvel at the, 25
master, 85
materials, 61
matter, 5, 17, 26, 43, 45, 57, 63, 65, 70, 76, 78, 79, 83, 87
matters, 7, 53, 65, 70, 79, 85
Maximus, 11, 82, 85
me to be, 9
meaning, 17, 36
meant, 5, 79, 82
measure, 25
member, 1
memory, 23, 53, 66
Menippus, 85
mentor, 9
message, 85
Meteores, 85
Middle Comedy, 85
minds, 4, 37, 44, 56, 61
misery, 14
mispronunciation, 10
mistake, 10, 51
mistakes, 3, 63
mixture, 52, 61
moderation, 78

moment, 13, 23, 26, 33, 39, 41, 46, 51, 57
money, 2
more than a, 18
mortals, 83
mother, 9, 34
mountain, 81, 82
mouse, 71
moves, 65, 77
multiplies, 58
Muses, 85
music, 85
musings, 86
mysteries, 72
nature, 17, 22, 26, 27, 28, 30, 34, 42, 49, 50, 51, 52, 57, 58, 62, 64, 66, 69, 70, 77, 79, 83
nature of the, 22, 57
needs, 75
neither good, 5, 57
Nerves, 85
no need to, 50
nobody, 5
nothing truly, 61
notion, 10
notions, 18, 78
numbers, 36
observe, 66
obstacle, 30, 53
obstacles, 21, 49, 52, 53
obstruct, 30
of all things, 33
of knowledge and, 86
of the body, 75
of the future, 75
officers, 2
operations, 29
opinion, 38, 51, 82
opinions, 15, 51, 57, 62
opportunity, 17, 49, 67, 75
order, 42, 61, 69, 71, 72
origin, 60, 83
others, 5, 6, 9, 13, 18, 21, 25, 26, 31, 35, 38, 43, 49, 51, 54, 56, 58, 62, 63, 64, 65, 66, 69, 73, 76, 84, 85, 87
our lives are, 59

overlook, 76
pages, 4
Palestra, 85
Pancratiast, 85
parents, 1
Parmularii, 85
part of life, 38, 43, 58
part of nature, 14, 30
part of the universe, 29
particle, 66
partnership, 5
parts, 25, 71
pass away, 30, 53
passed away, 1
passes, 59, 76
passion, 6
passions, 21, 61
peace, 3, 5, 6, 9, 13, 15, 27, 42, 57
peers, 72
people, 2, 3, 5, 6, 7, 8, 9, 10, 20,
    25, 28, 31, 34, 35, 37, 38, 39,
    45, 46, 52, 54, 55, 58, 59, 60,
    62, 68, 71, 72, 73, 77, 82
periods, 85
person, 2, 8, 9, 10, 30, 31, 39, 43,
    45, 63, 65
Phalerum, 83
Pheidias, 85
Philippus, 85
philosophers, 11, 27, 33, 67, 83
philosophy, 2, 5, 11, 27, 82, 84, 85,
    87
Phocion, 85
physicians, 84
physics, 83
picture, 43, 44, 49, 66
piety, 6
Pine, 85
place, 14, 19, 23, 26, 31, 36, 41,
    43, 45, 51, 61, 64, 67, 77, 82, 86
Plato, 81, 83, 85, 86
Platonics, 86
point, 75
polite, 6, 63, 66
Pompeii, 86
Pompeius, 86
possessions, 75

possibility, 7
power, 7, 14, 25, 30, 61, 68
power of the, 68
powerless, 29
practice, 19, 37
praise, 23, 61
prayers, 2
presence, 75
Prestidigitator, 86
pretentiousness, 10
principle, 4, 5
prioritize, 6, 17, 18
Priscus, 84
probability, 54
problems, 2, 59
process, 14, 56, 64
progress, 26, 67, 69
prosperity, 35
prudence, 14
pursuit, 86
Pyrrho, 86
Pythagoras, 86
Quadi, 2, 86
qualities, 6, 51, 63, 64
quality, 53
question, 29, 50
rationality, 65
reach, 36, 49
reality, 22, 51
reason, 4, 17, 22, 27, 38, 42, 51,
    54, 62, 67, 78
rebellion, 3
reference, 76
reflections, 6, 19
relationship, 61
relationships, 9, 46
religions, 7
reminder, 70
repay, 72
reputation, 5
resilience, 3, 21
resources, 42
respect, 11, 24, 30, 34
respond, 6, 10, 36
restraint, 53
result, 29
reverence, 33

rewards, 45, 46, 69
Rictus, 86
righteousness, 18, 23
Rome, 1, 2, 3, 38, 82
round, 17, 54, 85
route, 30
rules, 83
Rusticus, 10, 86
Sacrary, 86
sadness, 43
Salaminius, 86
Samos, 84, 86
Sarmatae, 86
satisfaction, 13
savor, 24
Sceletum, 86
school, 4, 9, 83, 84, 85, 86
schools, 86
Scipio, 86
search, 55
Secutoriani, 87
seeds, 64
seize, 49, 75
sense, 13, 42, 68, 77, 83
senseless, 14, 71
sensuality, 18
sentiment, 10
separation, 69
sequence, 36
settlement, 3
Sextus, 10, 87
share, 55, 58
shine, 55
should not be, 31, 37
shows, 6
siblings, 61
sides, 36
sights, 38
Silly, 87
silver, 61
simpletons, 37
simplicity, 8
sinners, 46
Sinuessa, 87
situation, 22
situations, 6, 7, 21
skills, 19, 37

smell, 68
sociability, 35
society, 11, 66, 83
Socrates, 7, 46, 72, 85, 86, 87
soldier, 81
soldiers, 86
someone, 6, 18, 30, 36, 43, 51, 56,
    67, 79
sooner, 60
sophists, 10
source, 37, 52, 86
speak, 10, 19, 71, 75
spectacle, 69, 82
speech, 52
spirits, 62
squabbles, 30
stands, 82
stars, 32, 37
state, 14, 60, 83
statesman, 83, 85
Stint, 87
Stoic, 4, 5, 7, 81, 82, 83, 85, 86, 87
Stoics, 3, 4, 5, 85
stones, 35
story, 2
stray, 23
strength, 5, 21
strings, 85
strive to be, 35
students, 4
success, 35, 39, 46, 63, 65
successor, 87
suspicion, 18, 85
swayed by the, 62
sweat, 52
Syracuse, 81, 83
system, 4
take a moment, 37
take a moment to, 37
take action, 51
take away, 67
take control, 13
tasks, 11, 52
teachers, 6, 9
teachings, 10, 33, 86
temperance, 11, 18
terror, 25

thanks, 11
the ability to, 33, 49, 69
the basis of, 70
the beauty of, 7, 17, 44
The Cynics, 83
the death of, 72
the grand scheme, 38
the laws of nature, 28
the most of it, 21, 75
the same fate, 61, 78
the source of, 52
the start and, 31
the world around, 5, 19, 30, 55
the world around you, 19, 55
the world as, 79
Theophrastus, 87
thing, 3, 15, 25, 31, 32, 35, 43, 50,
    67, 71, 75, 76
things, 2, 3, 5, 6, 7, 14, 18, 22, 25,
    26, 28, 29, 31, 34, 35, 36, 37,
    38, 39, 41, 42, 44, 46, 49, 50,
    53, 55, 58, 59, 60, 61, 62, 63,
    65, 66, 67, 70, 72, 75, 76, 77,
    78, 79, 86, 87
think of the, 64
those who are, 25, 59
thoughts, 5, 6, 7, 19, 23, 38, 39, 55,
    75, 77
Thrasea, 84, 87
threat, 8
Tiberius, 87
times, 5, 24, 27, 41
titles, 2, 85
to be kind, 11, 38, 63
to be so, 45, 67
to do so, 11, 29, 77
to do what is, 25, 29
to live a, 2, 10, 27
to live in, 87
to protect the, 3, 35
to the gods, 11, 18
to the gods and, 11
to your own, 59
today, 13, 52, 59, 83, 86
tolerate, 56
tools, 19, 27, 62
To-torn, 87

towards, 29, 67
track, 31
trade, 24
tragedy, 8
Trajan, 24, 87
transformation, 44, 50, 69
transformations, 30
translations, 8
treat, 24, 39, 54
trivialities, 64
trouble, 2, 9
true happiness, 8
trust, 12, 18, 41, 42, 52, 75, 76
truth, 4, 18, 19, 42, 67, 76
truths, 7, 22, 78
uncertainty, 57
vagaries, 75
value, 17, 30, 33, 38, 79
values, 17, 29, 53, 55, 61, 64
vanity, 57, 61
vastness, 21
Verus, 1, 2, 9, 84, 87
Vespasian, 24, 84, 87
vices, 62, 84
victim, 22
views, 77, 85
virtues, 62
wander, 56
warriors, 65
water, 61, 63, 66
wealth, 5, 6, 83, 85
what is good, 51
what your nature, 28, 49
wickedness, 41, 55, 59
will not be, 70
will soon be, 25
wisdom, 5, 11, 33, 59, 60, 61, 87
with one another, 12
with the divine, 4
words, 5, 75, 81, 82, 86
world, 4, 7, 9, 14, 22, 23, 24, 25,
    26, 27, 28, 30, 33, 41, 42, 45,
    49, 50, 52, 54, 57, 61, 63, 64,
    66, 68, 71, 72, 77, 78, 79, 85, 86
worry, 5, 18, 25, 29, 31, 51, 52, 53,
    54, 56, 61, 70
worse, 14, 70

years, 1, 2, 8, 46
you are part, 37
you can do, 18, 35, 43
you have the, 14
you will never, 18, 64

your life to, 23, 24, 45, 76
your life to the, 23, 24, 45, 76
your own judgement, 55
Zeno, 4, 87

* 9 786500 690842 *